C0-BJF-141

ERRATUM

The references to Harper & Row publication in 1974 of
LIFE IS REAL ONLY THEN, WHEN 'I AM' in the
footnotes to pages 16 & 17 are incorrect. No arrangements for publication of Gurdjieff's THIRD SERIES
have been completed.

IS THERE "LIFE" ON EARTH?

By the same author:

An Introduction to
Gurdjieff

J. G. Bennett

STONEHILL

First Printing

ISBN 0-88373-007-3 : Hardcover
0-88373-008-1 : Softcover
Library of Congress Catalog Card Number: 73-80673
Manufactured in the United States of America

First Published 1973

All rights reserved
including the right of reproduction
in whole or in part in any form.
Copyright 1949 & 1973 by J. G. Bennett
Published by the Stonehill Publishing Company,
a division of Stonehill Communications, Inc.
38 East 57 Street, New York City, 10022

Is There "Life" On Earth?

Prepared as a Series of Four Lectures, first delivered by Mr. Bennett at Denison House, London, on 3, 10, 17 & 24, October, 1949, under the name: "Gurdjieff—the Making of a New World."

Lecture 2, "Gurdjieff—the Man and his Work," has since been rewritten to include an account taken from a biographical note, prepared by some of Gurdjieff's older pupils at the request of his American publishers.

The Lectures have been otherwise revised only so that they may now appropriately relate in their tense to Gurdjieff, whose death occurred on 29 October, 1949, a few days after the presentation of the final Lecture.

An Introduction to Gurdjieff

INTRODUCTION

For at least ten thousand years, from the end of the Ice Age, the people of Central Asia were the active core of the human race. When India and the Far East, all of Europe, and all Africa except Abyssinia and what is now the Sahara Desert, were still in the hunting and fruit gathering cultures of the stone age, the Aryan, Turanian and Semitic people of Central Asia had highly developed societies and possessed knowledge of man, his nature and his true destiny that has never been surpassed. The region was protected by mountains on all sides to which about seven thousand years ago the deserts of Gob, Kizil and Kara Kum added further impediments to travel. The land was fertile and the climate envigorating and wave after wave of conquest and civilization have come from it through the millenia. Only a handful of travellers like Marco Polo, Ibn Battuta and Ch'ang Ch'un dared the perils of travelling through the mountains and brought back accounts of the high civilizations they found, but even they did not penetrate to the sanctuaries where the ancient wisdom was preserved. These were hidden in the great limestone caves of the Syr Darya and the Pianje rivers, in the remote valleys

11

An Introduction to Gurdjieff

of the Pamirs and the Hindu Kush and the oases of the Gobi and Takla Makam deserts. It was not until the 18th Century that the Russians began to penetrate from the West and systematically destroyed the old cultures.

Towards the end of the 19th Century, Helena Petrovna Blavatsky, co-founder of the Theosophical Society, claimed to have penetrated beyond Tibet and reached the sanctuaries of the Masters of Wisdom. Her books, *The Secret Doctrine* and *Isis Unveiled,* showed familiarity with the Tantric Buddhism of Tibet, but not of the far more remarkable teachings preserved in Central Asia. Nevertheless, her books and her personality aroused a deep and lasting interest in the belief that there are 'Masters' who influence the destiny of mankind from 'Shamballa', the supposed center of the earth's spiritual activity. Many travellers have tried unsuccessfully to trace the sources she claimed to have discovered but little that was convincing came out until Gurdjieff appeared on the European scene soon after World War I. When his pupil, P.D. Ouspensky, began to lecture in London and Gurdjieff soon after set up his Institute in Paris, it was quickly recognized by students of esoteric and spiritual teachings that something new and astonishing had reached us from the East. I was one of the few who had known Gurdjieff before he came to Europe for I first met him in Constantinople in 1920. I was already deeply interested in Central Asia and had met many Sarts, Uzbegs, and Turkmens on their way through Constantinople, among whom were Sufi sheikhs who were not ordinary men. Gurdjieff was in a

Is There "Life" On Earth?

class by himself. All of us who met him then soon realized that he must have penetrated more deeply than any previous travellers of the nineteenth and twentieth centuries into the secrets of the Masters of Wisdom. Since then more than fifty years have passed and more and more people are realizing that he had a message of real value to the modern world.

Gurdjieff was born on 28 December 1877. By the time he was eleven, he had shown unusual psychic gifts and had already decided to devote his life to finding an answer to the question: 'What is the sense and purpose of life on the earth and in particular of human life?' His early searches took him to Crete and the Holy Land, to Egypt, Abyssinia and Mesopotamia, to Kurdistan and North West Persia. From 1898 onwards he concentrated his search in Turkestan and the regions north of Tibet as far as China and Tibet itself. In the course of his travels he found traces of traditions thousands of years old and was able to enter and live in communities that were custodians of the tradition. He told us that he had met men over two hundred years old and in full possession of their faculties. He witnessed temple dances and rituals through which the ancient wisdom had been preserved. After many years of search he arrived unexpectedly at one of the sanctuaries of the Sarmán Brotherhood that was founded in Babylon at the time of Sargon the Great—that is, 4500 years ago—and was initiated into their secrets. During his time in Abyssinia and Egypt he had been able to decipher secrets of the Egyptian mysteries from the time before the Sphinx was buried in sand. In short, he was

An Introduction to Gurdjieff

privileged to receive help and instruction from Masters of Wisdom of whose very existence very few people are aware.

By the year 1909, his period of search was coming to an end and he set himself to find means of putting all he had learned and discovered for himself into a form that would make it accessible to ordinary people under the changed conditions of the modern world. In 1911, Gurdjieff set up his own center in Tashkent, the ancient Yesi. It is a remarkable tribute to the standing he had already acquired, that he was accepted as a new spiritual teacher in a place within reach of the great Syrdaryan caves and valleys which for thousands of years had been the home of the Masters of Wisdom. He remained in Tashkent for two years in which time he convinced himself that his 'system' would help people of many different types and races. He decided to move to the West and chose Moscow where he already had connections. He himself declared that this decision was taken in agreement with the Masters of a certain brotherhood who undertook to train helpers selected by him for the projected dissemination of his 'ideas'. In Russia he was received in the highest circles, even being presented to Tzar Nicholas of whom he always spoke in affectionate and admiring terms. His plans were delayed by the First World War and completely upset by the Russian Revolution. He went to the Caucasus and made a fresh start in Tiflis. He finally decided to abandon Asia and came to Constantinople in 1920 where I met him for the first time. He went on to Europe and founded his Institute for the Harmonious Development of Man at the

Is There "Life" On Earth?

Château du Prieuré south of Paris. I spent some time at the Institute in 1923 and had personal experience of his amazing psychic powers as well as of his profound knowledge of the laws of the universe and the nature of man.

He went to the U.S.A. in January 1924, when his lectures and demonstrations of temple dances and sacred gymnastics attracted much attention in the press and brought him both pupils and money. There was, however, little grasp of what it all signified. This was as much due to his strange behavior as to the novelty and difficulty of his ideas.

He had spoken to me in 1923 of his great plan to found branches of his Institute as well as small centers for study in all the chief countries of the West. I think he would have pursued this plan but for a nearly fatal automobile accident on 6 July 1924 soon after his return from America.

He then set himself to express his ideas and convey his methods through books. The next ten years, from 1925 to 1935, were largely spent in writing.

Meanwhile I had accepted him as my teacher and this relationship remained unchanged to the end of his life. I saw a great deal of him in 1948 and 1949 both in Paris and in New York. The lectures that form the present book were delivered only a week or two before his death in 1949. I last saw him on Sunday, 23 October, and spoke to him about the last lecture of the series that I was due to give the next day. He said that he counted upon the publication of his writings to spread his ideas far more widely than hitherto. He had given me copies of all the manuscripts. It was obvious

An Introduction to Gurdjieff

to me that he had prolonged his life at the cost of great suffering in order to make sure that his books would not only be published but made freely and widely available. Having failed in his great plan for establishing a world-wide organization based on the principles of the Fourth Way, Gurdjieff counted upon his writings to do the work for him after his death. The First Series under the title *All & Everything*[1] was published a few months later. The Second Series, *Meetings with Remarkable Men*[2], came out in 1957. The Third Series is now being prepared for publication this fall. When I was giving the lectures in London, I did not know what Gurdjieff intended to do with this unfinished work. Now that twenty-five years have passed, his family, that is the children of his brother, Dimitri, and his sister, Sophie Ivanovna, have decided that it should be published[3]. They have authorized me to quote a passage which shows Gurdjieff's intentions in writing it.

The four lectures which at the time I called "Gurdjieff—the Making of a New World" cannot be published under that title because it has already been registered for another book. The lectures themselves are fundamentally unchanged. I was naturally very tempted to rewrite them in the light of the extensive researches I have made into Gurdjieff's early life and the sources of his teaching, the resulting work of

1 *All and Everything:* "An Objectively Impartial Criticism of the Life of Man" or *Beelzebub's Tales to His Grandson*. Harcourt, Brace & Co. 1950; E.P. Dutton & Co., Inc. 1964.

2 *Meetings With Remarkable Men*. E.P. Dutton & Co., Inc. 1963.

3 *Life Is Real Only Then When 'I Am'*. Harper & Row, 1974.

Is There "Life" On Earth?

which will shortly be published[1], and also with hindsight of what has happened in the years since he died. I resisted this temptation because they express what I and many others were feeling at the time. We could not imagine that Gurdjieff was so soon to leave us. He was planning to revive his Institute at a Château near Paris and intended to go to America to raise the money required. He was already selecting people to live there. He was so adept at hiding his real feelings that I cannot tell if he knew that death was imminent or if he thought he could once again call upon his extraordinary powers to prolong his life. It may be that the decision was not taken until a week before the end.

The passage I am going to quote comes in the Introduction to Book I of the Third Series: *Life is Real Only Then When 'I Am'*.[2] He writes:

> Soon after I had chosen for myself this kind of activity, as the most corresponding to my unexpectedly arisen physical state, that is to say the profession of a writer, and when, parallel to the improving of my physical state, I clearly understood that, due to certain written explanations, namely my personal ones there will arise for the majority of contemporary people, as well as for the future generation a great benefit; this series of books was also predetermined by me to acquit myself consciously with Great Nature for my arising and existence, chiefly for an

[1] *Gurdjieff—Making A New World*. Harper & Row, 1974.
[2] Quoted from the forthcoming Harper & Row edition by permission of the family and heirs of Mr. Gurdjieff.

17

An Introduction to Gurdjieff

existence not merely as an 'ordinary-life', automatically fulfilling something necessary for general realizations of Great Nature, but as a determinate, conscious existence, impartially valuating itself and besides gifted with the capacity for an all–round perfecting, independent unity. . . .

For the readers of this series of my exposings, no matter to which degree of consciousness they should rank themselves, in my opinion, it would not be superfluous to know among other things, from which of my conceptions and instinctive suppositions derived the sentence used by me above 'to-acquit-myself-with-Great-Nature'.

This sentence which almost involuntarily burst forth from me, arose and taking a shape derived from the totality of my instinctive and conscious convictions, that by this act, that is to say, by exposing this third and last series of my writings, that I rely and hope to fulfil: firstly—the chiefest, in my opinion, duty of a man who has reached responsible age and which consists in preparing infallibly for posterity, according to one's individuality, certain profitable instructions; secondly—to justify worthily—this latter quite subjectively—the sense of all my past intentional labours and conscious renunciations of all kinds of benefits, crystallised generally in the life of contemporary people, which have always been very easily obtainable for me and

Is There "Life" On Earth?

finally, thirdly, in the moment of my last breathing, to experience with no possible mental, sensitive or instinctive doubt the impulse, sacred for a man, which was called by the ancient Esseis[1] "the–impartial–self–satisfaction."

This was written in Paris in 1933 when Gurdjieff's hopes of re-establishing his Institute were crumbling. Forty years later this 'edifyingly–instinctive' series of writings is to become available to all seekers.

Gurdjieff's message is clear. The human predicament cannot be resolved by exhortation or organization. It is no use telling us what to do if we cannot do it. It is equally useless to set up organizations whose members do not even know what has to be done. The way out is through the transformation of individuals who in their turn can guide and help mankind through the perils ahead. If we wish to take our part in this work we must be prepared not only to make sacrifices but to make intelligent sacrifices. It is not enough to be willing, we must also learn 'how to be'. We must set ourselves to understand the 'sense and purpose of our existence' and then devote ourselves to its realization. For both stages, we need to 'know--how'. My hope in publishing these four lectures is that they may encourage those who have come in contact with Gurdjieff at second or third hand to come closer to his work. It is now fifty-two years since I first met

[1] The manuscript reads "Esseis." This may be an error for either Essenes—or Essevis, a Sufi community that has existed in Central Asia for 900 years.

him and I am more than ever convinced that he has a
message of hope for this distressed world.

J. G. Bennett
Sherborne House
Sherborne, Glos., England

January 13th, 1973

1

THE NEEDS OF A
NEW EPOCH

1

THE NEEDS OF A NEW EPOCH

To enable me to come quickly to grips with the task I have set myself in these four lectures, I propose to take for granted that we are passing through a period of transition in human history when, in some sense, an old world is dying and when, therefore, in some sense, a new world must be born. You may conceive this transition as a relatively commonplace change from one set of social and material conditions of life to another. I shall ask you to let me assume that an event far more extraordinary is taking place—nothing less than the end of an epoch which has lasted for several thousand years, and the heralding of a new epoch in which human existence will be quite different from anything mankind can remember.

It is in this extreme sense that I originally chose as the title of this series of lectures, "The Making of a New World." I linked this with the name of "Gurdjieff," and my aim is to show you why I am convinced that it is in his teaching that the seeds of a new world are to be found.

First, we must agree as to the material of which such seeds are made. Here again I shall spare you a long discussion and say, without attempting to prove

23

An Introduction to Gurdjieff

it, that it is in the inner world of man, that is, by ideas, and not in his outer world, that is, by organization, that the life of man is changed. Obviously, not every idea has power to change our life. It is said that what a man thinks, that he becomes. Like so many pithy sayings, this contains much that is true, but also much risk of misunderstanding. In one sense, it is only too painfully true. If I allow myself weak, idle thoughts, I shall become a weak, idle man. If I allow myself thoughts which are egoistic, jealous, self-centered, I shall become an egoistic, jealous, self-centered man. Every meanness, every self-indulgence and every violent impulse that takes root in my inner world, will, sooner or later, find expression in my outer manifestations. Unfortunately, the converse is not true. I do not find that if I think noble thoughts or entertain fine projects in my mind, they have a corresponding effect on my behavior. I may decide to do admirable things, and yet find that, however much I may think about them, they do not get done.

We must therefore distinguish between the thoughts that act upon us while we remain passive and the thoughts which become effective only in so far as we ourselves give them force. We are enslaved by the thoughts which correspond to our weaknesses. If we allow ourselves to live in daydreams, we inevitably become idlers and dreamers. But if we want to achieve, it is not sufficient to think. We have also to put force into our thoughts. This is true not only for each of us as individuals, but also in the larger affairs of the world. We see the operation of both kinds of thoughts—suspicious, grasping thoughts, fearful

The Needs of a New Epoch

thoughts. These engender fear, suspicion and grasping behavior in groups of people and in the nations of the world. We also see very good intentions expressed and thought about very earnestly, but no corresponding results in the life of communities or the policies of nations.

If, then, it is not sufficient to have "good" ideas in order to achieve "good" results, how can ideas be the seeds of a new and better world? If we can find the answer to this question, we shall have learned one of the most important secrets of human destiny. History teaches us that the world is not changed by ethical precepts, however convincing to the mind. Nor, in the long run, does the arousing of moral emotions, however powerful in their immediate effect, give a permanent new direction to the course of human life.

I shall take one of the most fundamental of the ideas which have in various ways influenced the life of man. This is the *idea of choice*—that man is a being who is not, or at least need not be, a mere automaton, but a being who can contribute in some way to the determination of his own destiny. This is a very big idea and, if it is valid, it represents the most important distinguishing mark of a *man* as compared with a thing, or even an animal, in whom such a power does not reside. To have the power of choice is to be responsible not only for ourselves, but also for the effect of our actions upon other people. As an abstract idea, the responsibility of man is usually taken for granted, and most people would hold without question that it is applicable to them. Combining this with what I said about the noble thoughts which do

An Introduction to Gurdjieff

not issue in noble actions, you will understand that the abstract idea that we are beings endowed with the power of choice is not sufficient to produce a change in our lives. If we can choose to do what is right and wise, it is very strange that we do it so seldom. A sincere reflection on human behavior is enough to convince us that the power of choice plays much less part in the life of man than we think. It is very important that we should recognize and face this fact and try to understand its causes. They lie in the absence of force and urgency in our attitude towards choice.

If we look at the form in which the conception of choice has been put before mankind in the great religions of the world, we can see that it is always associated with some further idea which brings with it a sense of urgency. We find in Deuteronomy, "I have set before you life and death, blessing and cursing: choose therefore life that thou and thy seed may live." Here, the idea of choice is associated with that of life and death for ourselves and our children. You will see at once how great is the difference between asserting that man is free, and therefore responsible for his actions, and setting before him the choice between life and death. In the passage I have just quoted, choice refers to this visible life only and to the future of mankind. In the teaching of Gotama Buddha, the idea of causality occupies a central place, and man is represented as the slave of cause and effect, unless by his own choice he seeks and wins his own liberation. To be the slave of causality is to be condemned to unending suffering. He who sees this, and chooses to

26

be free, can win a state of bliss which is beyond description. In the Christian Gospels, choice is expressed in a still stronger form as that between the gaining or losing of eternal life.

I have cited these few examples to show how the idea of choice is reinforced in the great religious teachings. It is because of this added power that they have been able to change the course of history.

We can see from the history of the past two hundred years what happens when the idea of choice is shorn of any compelling motive. As the idea that man *must* choose degenerates into the belief that he *can* choose, and choose moreover as and when he himself wishes, it passes from a positive to a negative thought in the sense of the distinction which I made at the beginning of this lecture. If I think of my freedom as the right to satisfy my egoistic impulse, and not as responsibility towards Higher Power, the whole significance of my life changes. When this degeneration is almost universal, as it has become in our time, nothing remains to prevent mankind from drifting passively towards self–destruction.

If now we look more carefully at the idea of the power of choice, we can see it can be given two entirely different meanings. In one sense, it can mean ability to choose between alternative possibilities, both on the same level; for example, choosing which make I shall choose for my new car. In the other sense it means choosing between two different levels—for example, to choose between shirking or carrying out a difficult decision. It is one of Gurdjieff's great contributions to the clarification of human destiny that he makes us see the distinction between real choice and illusory choice. It is an illusion to think that I can choose which make of car I shall buy, for this is determined by causes which already exist, but there is a real choice between doing and failing to do something which goes against some strong impulses of my own nature, for the doing of it implies some degree of liberation from causality.

The distinction between real and illusory choice lies deep at the root of all the great religious teachings, but it has never been made sufficiently clear. What is, however, clear and explicit in all the great religions, is their teaching that man is confronted with the choice between life and death. There are two paths before him, one the easy path which goes by itself, each step determined automatically by what has gone before. The other path is difficult and can be taken only by paying the price of effort and sacrifice. It is the distinction between the wide gate and broad way that leads to destruction and the straight gate and narrow way that leads to life.

Now, because our nature is such that a great part of each one of us is inclined to easy things, we tend to soften the sharpness of the choice. So it comes about that in the course of time, every great teaching is watered down and weakened until it has no longer the power to make men act. When Gotama Buddha preached his doctrine of Dukkha, that is, suffering and the way to the cessation of all suffering, the idea had power and turned men's minds away from the easy doctrine of vicarious liberation through the ritual sacrifices of the Brahmins. A new force entered the world, not simply from the idea of liberation, but because this idea was given force by the example of the Buddha himself and the conviction which he was able to establish in men's minds that liberation was possible and that the price, however great, was worth paying. As generation succeeded generation, Gotama became a legend, the conviction engendered by his own demonstration that his way could be followed lost its force in the picture of a super-human being to whom such an achievement would be effortless, and so his life was robbed of its force as an example to ordinary men. The same has happened each time that the conception of salvation, so fundamental for human destiny, has been given a new form.

Let me try to show you how an idea can have power, because if we can be clear about that, we can understand something of the conditions under which something new and effective can enter the life of man. Let me take the idea of death. I do so because it occupies a central place in Gurdjieff's teaching and he has himself made use of it to demonstrate the very point I wish to make. The idea of death is a very big idea and one from which there is no escape. We are all of us mortal, and we all know that we must die. The idea of our mortality might therefore be expected in some way to affect our lives, but we know from our own experience and from all we see around us, that, on the whole, the idea of death plays little part except on the rare occasions when we are brought close to it.

But what happens when we are brought close to it? Let us try to make a picture for ourselves. Supposing that someone very close to me, without whom I

An Introduction to Gurdjieff

cannot imagine myself living, is not very well with a recurring fever. I decide to consult the doctor. He takes it rather seriously and advises me to go to a specialist. She goes to a specialist, as advised by the doctor, and he examines her, and asks to see me and begins asking me various questions which I know are irrelevant, and little by little, something begins to grip my heart, and I know what he is going to tell me. He tells me that she has an inoperable cancer, and has twelve months to live, but at the same time, he can do something for her which can relieve her present suffering, put off the time when she will be disabled, and she will for a number of months be able to live a normal existence. It is very important, therefore, if she is to have the utmost advantage of this respite, that she should not know about her disease, so he advises me that I should not let her know. I see in a flash the kind of future that lies before me. I must face what is going on, but at the same time I must hide it, and also I have to think that for this limited time I can no longer allow myself selfish actions and careless words that I allowed myself in the past. The memory that her death is inevitable reminds me constantly. In this way, the idea of death becomes powerful and affects my actions and enables me to do things which I could not have done before, restrain myself in things in which I could not have restrained myself before. But supposing I change the picture again a little. Supposing instead of some other person, it was I myself that was involved, and I was told, or accidentally found out, or insisted on being told, that I was the one who was to die. Then a different process would have taken place.

The Needs of a New Epoch

Everyone who has been in contact with many people who were dying or inevitably had to die within a certain period knows this, that although the fear of death may be present or accepted in some way outwardly, very nearly always there is an inward rejection of the idea of death, an inward feeling that somehow this is going to be different, it is not going to be the same for me as it has been for other people. There must be some way out. This is very very frequent. Why? Because this idea has now become too strong, there is too much force in it, and such as I am, I am unable to accept it. I am unable to live by it, unable to live with the actual acceptance of the fact that I am going to die in such and such a period of time.

I give this second picture to show you that it can happen that ideas can be too powerful, so powerful that people can no longer respond to them. Perhaps you know the saying in Hebrews: "Strong meat belongeth to them that are of full age, even those who by reason of use have their senses exercised to discern both good and evil."

I think I have said enough to remind you that there can be such power in ideas that they will take hold of us and change our lives in a way that, by our own decision, our own feeling of what ought to be, we ourselves are unable to do. Now, can something similar enter into the life of man in general? We can see in the world round us that a change is needed, that the good intentions of people are not sufficient to bring about a good future for mankind. Most of us think very hard about the future. We see the danger of

31

war, and realise very well that another war would be so great a disaster that perhaps mankind would not recover from it. We see how, all over the world, the grasping for purely material conditions, the conception of life in terms of purely material values, is making the whole economic system of the world shake and perhaps collapse. We see also great deterioration in the lives of individuals, in human relationships, in family relationships and so on. We struggle against this. We think this a terrible thing—the increasing incidence of insanity and nervous disorder, the general neurasthenia of the world, the lack of harmony in family life. We know well enough that things must change or the future is very black, but how can change come? We must assume that it can come, otherwise it is useless to meet and talk about it. What does it mean, to change the future? Here we have one of the elements of new ideas which are possible. Two thousand five hundred years ago, in the time of Gotama Buddha whom I have mentioned already, there was, probably for the first time, clearly introduced into human thought the conception of causality and the inevitability of the causal sequence. This was a great thought, clearly formulated: "Out of this, that arises, and from the disappearance of this, that ceases to be." This thought had a very big effect, because there previously had been a widespread feeling that any sort of miracle, any sort of preternatural happening was possible. The new idea was very sobering. But side by side with it, another idea was introduced, that escape from this general law of causality was also possible. If there was an inward

The Needs of a New Epoch

change in man, he could liberate himself entirely from it. The doctrine of liberation was the essence of Gotama's teaching and it had great power at the time, but the idea of causality later became very artificial and within a very few generations, it was replaced by other ideas and watered down and lost sight of until it re-entered western thought as a philosophical or scientific principle. In our western world, it has become a very important factor, because with the progress of what we call science with our exact measurements of physical processes, our understanding or knowledge of the quantitative aspect of the exchanges of energy and so on, we see that this is a universal law. And this has led people to think that the whole universe is just a mechanism, in which every thing is entirely determined. Many think that this is an inescapable conclusion—and it is indeed an inescapable conclusion if we confine ourselves to physical processes. An impartial study of the results arrived at by careful measurement and observation can allow us no doubt. When in physical science what was called the *Indeterminacy Principle* made its appearance, it looked as though there was some loophole, but this loses its meaning as soon as large systems enter, and the mechanistic universe remains just as inevitable as before. At the same time, quite untouched by these scientific conclusions, the feeling exists in man that somehow his choice is not just an illusion, he is not just a helpless spectator of things that are happening without the participation of his intention. I suppose this is not a very serious conflict for most people, and they do not feel it matters one way or another,

An Introduction to Gurdjieff

because life has to be lived just the same. It is only important in one sense, that it helps us to see what is the meaning of this principle which I formulated at the beginning of this lecture, that is, the principle that man is a being confronted with choice, before whom there are two different kinds of lives. Man is just a machine among machines, but a machine which can be free, can be not a machine. This would not be possible if there were not different levels of existence. On one level of existence, man is a machine living among machines; on another level of existence, there is the possibility of freedom. There are two worlds open to man, not one world far away and one here, but two worlds both here.

Just before the passage I quoted from Deuteronomy, are these verses:

> For this commandment which I command thee this day, it is not hidden from thee, neither is it far off.

> It is not in heaven, that thou shouldest say, Who shall go up for us to heaven, and bring it unto us, that we may hear it, and do it?

> Neither is it beyond the sea, that thou shouldest say, Who shall go over the sea for us, and bring it unto us that we may hear it and do it?

> But the word is very nigh to thee, in thy mouth and in thy heart, that thou mayest do it.

The Needs of a New Epoch

This was very rightly formulated, but how can it become a powerful idea, an idea which makes people act? Only if they can be convinced of the reality of these two worlds and of the complete difference between existence in one world and existence in the other world. Is it possible that people should be convinced of such a thing? This is where I can begin to speak about Gurdjieff's ideas.

He studied, and as I will tell you in later lectures, made it one of the tasks of his life to try to understand why we live on the earth, what purpose human life serves. You might have thought that this is one of the questions which would most occupy people, but on the whole it does not occupy them very much, and because they have not thought seriously about it and found a convincing answer, they have missed a good deal which can help them to live their lives. Here, I am only going to state, without explaining, and certainly without trying to prove, what it is that he, Gurdjieff, conceived to be the role of man in the universe—what we exist for. He says we exist to serve a two-fold purpose. The first purpose we must serve, whether we like it or not, in common with every other living being, whether animal, plant or anything else—and this purpose is to serve in the transformation of energy which is required for the whole cosmic economy particularly the economy of our solar system, our earth and our moon.

We all know that our bodies are like a chemical factory. We take in certain raw material, food and air, and so on. Out of this we make the material from which our bodies are built, and also the material from which our various kinds of experience become possible. Gurdjieff adds that, in addition to this, we also produce, release and make available a certain energy required for cosmic purposes. This corresponds to what I called earlier the mechanical line, and it corresponds to what is called in the Gospel the wide gate and broad way which leads to destruction, into which many go. We are all living for the same sort of purpose as animals live, thinking, it is true, experiencing, feeling, writing books, reading books, and organizing the world and so on, but still doing it all on that level, merely being a transformation station for energy. This is one inevitable destiny which no man can escape, one purpose for which he, and every other living thing, was made. But at the same time, man can, while serving this purpose, also serve another purpose, in which he can find a different destiny for himself and have a different value objectively. That can come about only if, in this process of transforming energy, he increases the efficiency or the amount of production so that he does what is necessary for him to do; he pays his debt, as it were, and has a surplus over for himself. This is simply another way of formulating the same principle I have spoken about several times, the choice between life and death. It is the principle of the straight gate and narrow way against the broad gate and wide way, or the same principle as formulated in the words, "the axe is laid at the root of the tree and the tree that does not bear fruit is hewn down and cast into the fire." The primary purpose of the tree is firewood, and the purpose more significant to the tree and more significant objectively is to bear fruit. The same concept arises in Buddhism through "The Four Noble Truths."

From our experience however, and from the study of history, we see that in fact, although these things have been taught in the past, they have no longer the power to affect the life of man. There are many reasons for this, but we will not consider them here. There are two extreme tendencies—one is to believe too much and too easily, the other is to believe too little. The result is that of the two possible destinies for man, people only see one and so lose the most important impulse to right action. They either say: "There is nothing more for man than this existence here, and he must make the best of it," or else they say, "He is immortal and bound in some way or another to go beyond this existence. Every individual is significant and valuable, even if he does very little about it." On the whole, those who adopt a religious conception of man tend to take the optimistic view that all will be well, providing he pays reasonable attention to certain rules, certain requirements. This is, of course, quite contrary to the teaching of all the Founders of religion, whose teaching is always of the nature of "many are called but few are chosen," but because of the tendency of people to take the rosiest view they can of a situation, this kind of severe conception of human life tends to be watered down; and if people are unable to take the rosy view, they go to the other extreme, which also dispenses them from

An Introduction to Gurdjieff

very serious efforts. They say, in effect: "There is nothing more in it; come, let us eat, drink and be merry, for tomorrow we die. Let us look after at least the material necessities, if not our own, at any rate the material necessities of those who are in want. This is all we can expect out of life, and all that life can expect out of us." Between these two kinds of views, the whole future of mankind is drifting into disaster, because neither of them corresponds to reality and neither of them produces in man the one response which is essential, not only for his own personal welfare, but for him to fulfill the high purpose for which he exists. The right response is that he must make efforts, struggle to raise himself above this level of mechanical existence, to lift himself out of this causal mechanism; or, putting it in different terms, he must make for himself a soul, he must make himself an independent, free being; he must make himself, in other words, something which he is not; and he can only do that if the necessity for it appears to him with power, with force.

I have quoted from Mosaic, Buddhist and Christian sacred books, and I could have quoted also from the Upanishads, from the Koran, or from the writings of saints and mystics of all ages. I could have shown you how the doctrine of choice between life and death, between the supremely valuable and the worthless runs like a golden thread through them all. Hearing me, you may well be tempted to ask what need there is then of a new world. Should not our aim be rather to restore what has been well understood and powerful in men's lives in the past, rather than seek for a new

The Needs of a New Epoch

teacher and a new gospel? In one sense, it is true—and Gurdjieff himself always emphasized it in his teaching and in his writing—that the truth about human destiny has been understood and the way of life followed far better in the past than in our time. I think that I have said enough to make the answer clear. What we lack is not the idea in the sense of knowledge of what should be done, but the *Idea* in the sense of the living force which makes that knowledge effective in our actions. Those of us who have studied Gurdjieff's teaching have felt in it, above all, the force which drives to action and the sense of urgency which makes it possible to pay the price without waiting till tomorrow.

It is very difficult for people brought up in the environment of western thought to experience the true sense of choice between life and death which presents itself to man. We are professedly Christian peoples, and the teaching of Jesus Christ, as preserved for us in the Gospels, states the choice without compromise. But Christianity as we know it is not the teaching of Jesus Christ, but the distorted remnants which have survived the falsifications of Greece and the power politics of Rome. Gurdjieff adds in his discussion of Christianity the further baneful influence of what he calls the "Babylonian dualism" expressed in the doctrine of 'heaven' and 'hell'. This idea for a time had great power over the minds of men, but it does not correspond to reality, and it has long ceased to be a dominating factor in human behavior.

The power of Gurdjieff's teaching lies in the elimination of everything fictitious and the return to

An Introduction to Gurdjieff

the naked reality of human destiny. The choice between life and death is not a matter of another life in which we only half believe. It is the ever present situation of every moment in the life of man. It is the choice between misery and rejoicing, between the immediate experience of life and the emptiness of no experience at all. It is the choice between helplessness and strength. When we turn our attention outwards towards the suffering and bewilderment of mankind, it is the choice between the sense of frustration and the confidence that something effectual can be done. In contemplating our own personal destiny, it is the choice between the doubt whether our life has any meaning and the certainty that, in the scheme of things, we have a necessary part to play. In the face of death, it is the choice between the terror of a wasted life that cannot be redeemed and the peace and satisfaction of him who quits the scene with his debts paid and his duty done.

On what does all this turn? What is the real meaning of this choice? These questions can only be answered if we understand Gurdjieff's teaching about the actual and the potential nature of man. We exaggerate to the point of absurdity the value and the powers of man, such as he is, and we underestimate and misconceive the almost unlimited possibilities of achievement for the man who follows the path of self-creation. The starting point of Gurdjieff's teaching is that man as we know him is a machine, controlled by external influences. He has no power of effective action. Nothing in his life is determined by his own will and choice. This is an assertion very difficult to accept,

The Needs of a New Epoch

and for many. it is the greatest obstacle in the way of approach to Gurdjieff's teaching. We are so thoroughly saturated with the notion of our ability, within limits, to do what we decide, that the assertion of our complete helplessness seems either ridiculous or disheartening. Nevertheless, it is true and can be established by each one of us beyond all doubt, if we are prepared to observe impartially our own behavior, or simply take into account the well-known facts of the working of the human nervous system and the chemistry of the human body. Our nervous system is a mechanism which reacts to external influences just as a typewriter types when the keys are worked. Many of you have no doubt read Sir Charles Sherrington's *Rede* Lecture on the "Integrative Action of the Nervous System," and will remember how he compares the mechanism of our behavior to a lock which is fitted by the nervous system like a key; and if we ask the question, "What turns this key?" he answers, "The external world."

There is nothing in man as we know him which is capable of independent, self-determined action. That is the picture of the "man machine" as Gurdjieff calls him, and before we can understand anything objectively about human nature and human destiny, we have first to recognize that this is a true picture. A strange situation exists today. It is widely said, especially by scientists and medical men, that man is a machine in the sense I have just described, and yet the very people who make this assertion entertain prejudices, make demands and themselves behave as though they and all other men were free beings,

An Introduction to Gurdjieff

responsible for their actions. They criticize and judge other people, and even become indignant over behavior which, according to their own theory, is not the result of any intention and could not be otherwise than it is.

It is no easy task to convince oneself or to convince others that men are machines, and yet this simple truth provides the only possible explanation of human behavior as we observe it, whether individually or in the mass. As we survey the life of man, we must see that it cannot be accounted for in terms of intentional, voluntary action. People do what they never intended, and, what they intend, they do not do. This applies just as much to those who are called strong, successful people as to unsuccessful, weak people.

When man first sees the reality of this situation face to face, he can scarcely escape from a feeling of terror as he looks forward into his own future. He sees that his life must of necessity be determined by the combination of external circumstances which chance or fate will bring. He is bound to drift helplessly through the stream of events in which he is immersed. If the stream threatens to bear him to destruction, he has no power to escape from it. Then and then only can the idea of self-creation begin to have power over him. He dare not remain such as he is.

In what I have just been saying, I have presented Gurdjieff's teaching in terms of this life only. I did so because we have in this life all the evidence that is needed to demonstrate that it is disastrous madness to neglect the work of self-creation. Gurdjieff's teaching is not, however, confined to the experience of this life only. The choice between life and death takes its sharpest and most urgent expression in contemplating the cessation of our own existence. It is true that all principles of self-creation would apply, even if the prospect which we contemplate stops short with our old age and our death. Gurdjieff asserts, on the basis of evidence of which I shall say a little in the later lectures, that the man who does not work for the creation of his own being has, and can have, no life but this; but the man who works and struggles for his own perfection has latent powers which are not confined to this visible life. When we go beyond the visible, facts in the ordinary sense are lacking. Facts there are, but they are all of such a nature that they cannot be established by processes in this mechanical level of existence about which I spoke. People who imagine that facts can be established in this mechanical level (e.g. in the so-called evidence of spiritualism), just do not see the alternative explanations. At the same time, facts can be established, but only on a different level of existence and a different level of experience. This I cannot either ask you to accept, nor can I here explain it in any detail. I am only adding it for completeness of the picture, because, sooner or later, there has to re-enter effectively into the life of man the idea that he is born with the possibility of living after death, not with the guarantee of it. He is born with the possibility of survival, and of a very great degree of further progress, and of serving a very high purpose—providing he makes use of this possibility which exists in his life, the possibility of producing by his own efforts a surplus of the energy which in any case is required of him. Whether he likes it or not, he has to restore the talent which was given to him, but if he will work and make something in addition, not only can he have something for himself, but be of different value, not only to his fellow men, but also to higher purposes. This is a fundamental conception. Let us see if I can put it succinctly.

Gurdjieff taught that man is a being with two destinies, one unavoidable, the other which it is in his power to have, but only if he himself earns it. And this second destiny, both as regards this life and any possibilities of another life, is incomparably more valuable than the first. As things are in the world at the present time, a very small proportion of people are doing anything effective for the attainment of the second destiny. This has certain very bad consequences, because the amount of this energy or matter which has to be produced in the life of man is determined not by himself, but by general influences. Suppose that we had a flock of sheep and required so much wool. If the sheep began to produce less wool, we should have to increase our flock. The population of the world is increased in very much the same way as the number of sheep that have to be kept as the wool deteriorates in quality and quantity and this carries with it very unsatisfactory consequences for mankind.

If what I have been saying is right, if it is, in fact, important to us individually and important to our race as a whole and to higher purposes also, that a sufficiently large number of people should struggle for the attainment of the second destiny, for living in the second world, then how is the necessity for this to be more widely felt? If it can be more widely felt, then future generations will enter into a new world. If not, they will not even keep the old world that we have known. It is about the answer to that question that I am going to speak in the next three lectures.

It may help you to understand something of the significance of these Ideas, for the future of mankind, if we try to visualize the effect on human relationships of a widespread realization that a man who does not struggle to attain a high destiny is no more than an animal, and, indeed, to be despised, which an animal is not. This is as far removed as possible from current ways of looking at people. They are valued for what they have, whether personal attractions or material possessions, for the position they occupy in life, and for similar factors which may have no connection at all with any true value. If once it is understood that the one true criterion which objectively decides the value of a man is his ability to struggle with himself, then only those would be respected who showed by their lives that they had achieved some measure of success in this direction. Their advice and help would be sought after, as people who had to some extent freed themselves from the mechanicalness of ordinary existence, from slavery to external things, from inner weakness. Ambition, the desire for power, fame, admiration, and the other motives which lead people to work and strive for positions of authority, would be seen as defects and weaknesses unworthy of a true man. The world would seek for teachers, rather than rulers, for those who could set an example rather than those who dominate and impress. The idea of a ruler who is himself the helpless slave of his own passions and his own automatism would be seen for what it is—a ludicrous travesty of a true master of men.

A further inevitable consequence would be the disappearance of the mutual misvaluation among different castes or classes and between nations and races. Such misvaluation is only possible so long as artificial values dominate the mind of man. Wars of aggression and conquest, ideological and religious wars, all have their origin in false conceptions of what is important for man. It will be by no means obvious to you if I say that only an understanding of the two-fold destiny of man can put an end to war. I propose, therefore, to finish this lecture by saying a little about Gurdjieff's teaching on the subject of war, its origin and the possibility of its ceasing.

Our attitude towards war is altogether false. We tend, as a matter of course, to regard war as the result of the intentional action of some wicked man or group of men or of some nation with a lust for conquest and power. Wars appear, to both sides engaged in them, as defence against some aggression, or as necessary for the furthering of some worthy, or even sacred, cause. Even those who most detest war and are prepared to sacrifice their liberty, or even their lives, to save themselves from becoming involved in it, conceive it as a wicked action, deliberately undertaken.

In reality, war is not like this at all. It is a terrible madness which overtakes mankind, when people lose even the little sense of reality they usually have. War is the supreme manifestation of human helplessness.

The Needs of a New Epoch

This applies to all forms of mutual destruction, whether revolution and civil war within a nation, or armed conflict between nations and the peoples of the world.

War has a twofold origin. The first is outside of man and arises independently. The second is within man and is due to his own weakness and failure. From time to time a special state of tension arises on the earth, which Gurdjieff calls the state of "Solioonensius." This state of tension arises from the relations between the planets. I do not mean by this that it is something supernatural or mysterious. It is a perfectly natural process, connected with the changes in the balance of electrical and other energy in the solar system. For example, it is already suspected by science that the occurrence of sun spots has an effect upon the human psyche.

It may help you to understand what I mean by calling Solioonensius a perfectly natural process, if you consider a simple phenomenon, well-known to all. I refer to the effect in Great Britain of the east wind, or in the Mediterranean of the Sirocco. When the east wind blows, people become irritable and nothing seems to go right. I once became interested in this because I wanted to see whether it was a real or an imaginary effect. I asked a number of people to observe carefully and let me know, as objectively as possible, whether they could detect a state of inner tension caused by the east wind. Nearly everyone confirmed that a state of irritability did, in fact, arise in them even before they were aware that the east wind was blowing. In a more subtle and pervasive manner,

An Introduction to Gurdjieff

great regions of the earth's surface, and sometimes even the whole of the earth, become subject to a state of tension which produces in people a strong sense of dissatisfaction with their conditions of life. They become irritable or aggressive, apprehensive, nervous and highly suggestible. Gurdjieff said that knowledge of Solioonensius existed thousands of years ago, and that he took the term from a very ancient tradition. At the present time, its significance has been forgotten or lost. The point is that there are two completely different ways in which people can react to a state of Solioonensius. It always arouses dissatisfaction, but this may be external or internal. External dissatisfaction leads to external conflict, internal dissatisfaction strengthens the desire to struggle with oneself. Those who understand the necessity for working on themselves and achieving the second destiny, find in that state of tension the greatest possibility of incentive and force to make them work harder. But those who do not have this feeling—this realization—project outwards their dissatisfaction and become hostile and angry with other people—suspicious, jealous, and the rest of it—and then, defenceless against these mass psychoses, begin to hate. And the very people who, only a few years before, could not conceive of themselves consenting to the idea of war, become involved in the destruction of other people. And those other people, passing through the same mass psychosis, with the same justification, wish in turn to destroy their existence.

It is possible, by careful study of history and of various psychological processes, to verify this. And,

48

The Needs of a New Epoch

once you understand it, you will see that there is no way by which war can be stopped other than by making people understand the necessity for this work. Otherwise, they have no defence against this state of tension; no contrivances, no organization, no good resolutions can avail, because there is a physico—chemical process involved. This state of tension must produce this result. We do not know when such a state of tension will come over the world again. When it is absent, we do not feel war as something possible, but when it approaches, nothing can be done unless an idea can come into the world which can act on a sufficiently large number of people to enable them to turn this force in a different direction. This is one reason why the change—the transition period from one epoch to another, from one world to another—is a dangerous period. Old ideas have lost their momentum and can no longer move the world. New ideas have not yet gained momentum. All through history, and even before the beginning of history, we find such periods accompanied by war and revolution; not because war and revolution are inevitable in themselves, but because people have lacked that discrimination which would enable them to use this situation rightly. If we are able to go into a world in which this is understood, then the course of history can be different, because the destiny of all mankind can be raised to a higher level. There is no higher purpose in the life of man than to bring about this great transition.

If a New World is to come we must first create it in ourselves. You may ask how the work of a few people

An Introduction to Gurdjieff

can change the world. It has always been so. Ideas are powerful, not organizations. Nothing can be done by outward force—everything can be done by inner strength. Let me try to give you a picture of how such changes can come. Some of you no doubt are cooks and have had to make sauces. Suppose I am making some sauce, like a hollandaise, which is liable to demulsify—that is, the butter separates from the egg. This can be a terrifying experience if you are making a sauce for sixty or seventy people with pounds of butter and dozens of eggs. An inexperienced cook loses his head and beats the sauce violently—but only makes things worse. A good cook pours a little water at one edge of the bowl and stirs quietly until it turns back again, and then it spreads through the whole mass until the sauce is right again. The first time you do this, it seems almost miraculous. It is the same with the world. Everywhere people are stirring violently to get oil and water to mix. This cannot happen. The part of wisdom is to establish, here and there, centers in which right relationships can exist by the power of a common understanding of what is ultimately important. From such centers there can spread throughout the world—perhaps far more quickly than you might imagine possible—the seeds of a new world.

I have said nothing yet about Gurdjieff himself. Next, I will speak about his life and work. You may have understood from what I have said why I am convinced that in his teaching we have the seeds of a new world. Even so, I should not leave you to infer, but should say clearly, why it is that, according to my understanding, his teaching has such a unique significance. No teaching can be divorced from the teacher. Abstract, impersonal ideas, can never have power. If Gurdjieff in his life had not exemplified his own teaching, and if he had not shown that it is possible to go by the way he had revealed, his teaching, however convincing to the mind, and however powerful in its emotional appeal, would have lacked the one essential element which can give force to an idea. A world on the brink of disaster, unable to believe and not daring to hope, has need above all of a guide who, with confidence, will give a lead and show a way which he is himself prepared to take. Gurdjieff has died, leaving the world the example of a life lived without compromise in terms of the ideas which are his legacy to the world.

2

GURDJIEFF—
THE MAN AND HIS WORK

2

GURDJIEFF—
THE MAN AND HIS WORK

My task now is to give you some account of Gurdjieff's life and work. My sources of information are, in part, his own autobiographical writings, and, in part, what I heard from him personally in conversation. For the story of his last thirty years I have been able, to some small extent, to draw on my own personal experience.

To start with, I must try to give you some picture of Gurdjieff's own country—that is, the Southern Caucasus. It is not easy for one who has not lived in the Near and Middle East to form a picture of the extraordinary mingling of races, religions and cultures, some very ancient, some relatively modern, which makes the Caucasus region almost unique on the earth. Waves of civilization have reached the Caucasus from North, South, East and West. It is like the high water mark on the seashore left by the tide where children playing at collecting shells and seaweed know that they will find the strangest treasures. West European, Slavonic, Turkish, Roman, Greek, Central Asian, Persian, Hittite, Babylonian and Sumerian cultures, together with others so ancient that their origin is unknown, have in turn

An Introduction to Gurdjieff

swept up to the Caucasus and then receded, leaving behind them living remains which have persisted to the present day. Not only this, but the collapse of civilizations has also been followed by migrations of peoples from the great rivers, the Tigris and the Euphrates, the Volga and the Oxus, which have further enriched the Caucasus with the traditions of ancient centers of culture. We have nothing in Europe comparable to this region, where dozens of races speaking many languages, some almost unknown, preserve the remains of former cultures and old customs which carry one back into the distant past of the human race.

Gurdjieff was born in Alexandropol near the Persian frontier of Russia on 28 December 1877. His own family came from the Ionian Greeks of Caesarea who have a continuous history dating back before the Christian era. The Greeks of Caesarea have preserved their culture through centuries of foreign rule and have a spirit of independence which aroused the admiration of all those who saw them as I did after the exchange of populations between Greece and Turkey in 1925. In the sixteenth century, some of the Greek families of Caesarea withdrew towards the north–east after the overthrow of the Byzantine Empire and among them were Gurdjieff's ancestors. They were what we should now call ranchers, that is, owners of great herds of sheep and cattle. In the middle of the last century they left Turkey for the Russian Caucasus.

After the Russo–Turkish War of 1877, his father, who had lost his herds through an epidemic of cattle

Gurdjieff—The Man and His Work

disease, established himself as a carpenter in Kars, which was then an important Russian military center near the Turkish frontier. In Kars entered one of the great influences of Gurdjieff's early life, when a saintly man, Father Borsch, Dean of the Military Cathedral, who had known him as a young chorister, offered that he should make himself responsible for the boy's education. Gurdjieff was taught by priests and doctors, in accordance with his father's plan that he should prepare himself for what he and the Dean conceived as a single vocation—to be physician for the body and confessor for the soul.

The boy himself was interested in mechanics and in natural and medical science—above all, in psycho-neurology. He also delighted in the acquisition of skill in every kind of manual trade. Nevertheless, the strange environment of the Caucasus, combined with several unusual experiences which pointed to the existence of supernatural forces in the life of man, turned his mind towards the conflict between the materialism of western science, which he valued for its methods of accurate observation and measurement, and the evidence of phenomena of which science was powerless to give an account. He was also steeped in the old traditions preserved in the ballads and sagas of the Asiatic bards. His father was himself a bard, famed for his knowledge of the legends of the ancient Assyrian and Sumerian cultures. In later life, Gurdjieff was deeply impressed by the discovery of cuneiform inscriptions which showed the accuracy with which these poems had been preserved through thousands of years.

An Introduction to Gurdjieff

He began on his own to visit the ruins of ancient cities and made archaeological discoveries which convinced him that in some former epoch, mankind had possessed knowledge, since lost, of the true sense and purpose of human life and the way to its fulfilment. He resolved to devote himself to the search for the reality underlying the seeming contradictions in the facts he had encountered. He could find no solution in western science and philosophy, or in the teachings of any of the Christian Churches or Moslem sects with which he had come in contact. Nevertheless, evidence accumulated that the knowledge and the way he was seeking might have been preserved in isolated communities. He made up his mind to travel and search until he should find the truth for himself.

Barely grown to manhood, he collected round him a handful of young men inspired with the same convictions and hopes. Together they formed a small society which styled itself the "Seekers of the Truth." Singly, or in twos and threes, they succeeded in visiting the countries where they hoped to find traces of real knowledge. In the course of their journeys, they met a number of remarkable men who joined them in their search and, with their experience and material resources, greatly extended the scope of their enquiry. Their travels took them far into Africa, through Persia, Turkestan, Tibet, India and the Far East, the Indonesian Archipelago, and even as far as Australia. They also travelled in little known parts of Europe, visiting monasteries and other places where ancient traditions might be preserved. Their travels were, from time to time, interrupted to enable them to take stock of what each had found. They kept abreast of the progress of western science—particularly astronomy, chemistry, medicine and psychology.

Gurdjieff tells us in his writings that, as time went on, he became more and more engrossed by what he calls the "idée fixe of his inner world"—namely the need to understand the sense and significance of human existence. Man, as he saw it, must, by his existence, serve a Great Purpose, and this purpose must equally be served by all. He was convinced that western philosophy was very far from understanding this Great Purpose—but he found the popular theories current in the East equally unsatisfying.

The thirst for an understanding of this central problem of human life was shared by the other members of the "Seekers of the Truth." As time went on, they found it possible to penetrate to places quite inaccessible to the ordinary traveller. They met many extraordinary men, sometimes individual dervishes or monks, sometimes whole brotherhoods or communities possessing, in varying degrees, insight into the nature of man and the secrets of human destiny. They were shown practical methods, transmitted from remote antiquity, for the development of the latent powers of man.

The journeys of the "Seekers of the Truth" came to an end before 1908. Some of them joined and remained in one or other of the brotherhoods they had succeeded in reaching; others had died. They had found personal guidance and help in their own search for an understanding of the meaning and purpose of their own existence. But they had also accumulated

An Introduction to Gurdjieff

data which showed the force of the ancient traditions and the extent to which the fundamental problems of Man and the Universe had been understood in the remote past. Having, at the same time, an intimate knowledge of western traditions and modern science, they were able to weld them all together into a single system of Ideas. There is no doubt that in this work, Gurdjieff was the leading spirit and driving force.

Before ending my account of this period of Gurdjieff's life, I must refer to strange and persistent personal misfortunes which seem to have formed an integral part of his destiny. To an unusual extent, his life was, again and again, endangered by accident and disease. No traveller entering into close contact with the populations of Eastern cities or with the insect-ridden valleys of Asia, from the Maeander to the Yangtze, can hope to avoid infection. Gurdjieff contracted nearly all the diseases of the East. These, he has said, left their permanent marks on his bodily organism. He has also described how three times he was almost killed by accidental bullet wounds in the early skirmishes in some war, first in Crete, then in Tibet, and, the third time, in the Caucasus in the fighting between Cossacks and Gurians. Later, automobiles took the place of bullets and he was several times nearly killed in motor car accidents. His life was always an alternation of intensive activity, with enforced stoppages due to accident and illness. No one who met him can doubt that his immense force was derived, in part at least, from his almost unceasing struggle with bodily suffering.

With the dispersal of the "Seekers of the Truth,"

Gurdjieff—The Man and His Work

Gurdjieff conceived it to be his own task to make known to the world the knowledge they had discovered. He had come more and more to realize the helplessness of modern man, having become the plaything of forces he had invoked, but could in no way control. He saw this helplessness as universal, pervading equally the East and the West. But against this, he could set his own conviction that the world could be saved from a terrible succession of disastrous wars and revolutions, of economic and social catastrophes, if only the right understanding of human destiny could again be introduced into the life of man.

He realized that, to carry through such a task, many helpers and much money would be needed. He set himself, for the first time in his life, the primary aim of accumulating wealth. He engaged in commerce and finance—public works contracting, buying and selling of businesses, development of oil fields. He also applied his immense knowledge of the human organism to the cure of drug addicts and dipsomaniacs, often being paid very large sums by rich families to undertake an apparently hopeless case.

I should refer here to his extraordinary powers of work. At several periods in his life he worked for months with only two or three hours sleep each day. This he did even when in bad health or when not fully recovered from an accident. No one associated with him in one of these periods of furious activity could understand how he was able to produce such personal energy for himself and such driving force behind others.

By 1912, he was by all standards a rich man and his

work had become known in many circles. He decided to lose no more time, but to found in Moscow an organization which he called the "Institute for the Harmonious Development of Man according to the Ideas of G. Gurdjieff." He started work with several groups of students, each specializing in one aspect of the work he wished to undertake. Some were engaged in psychological work, others in the study of the plastic arts and music. He also devoted particular attention to medicine and the chemistry of the human body. For these activities, he purchased and equipped a large estate near Moscow. He had recently married a Polish lady of the well-known Ostrovsky family and they decided to make their home in Russia.

Then came the First World War. Despite increasing difficulties, he continued his work in Moscow and even extended it to St. Petersburg, but concentrated more upon psychological work than upon scientific experiments. In 1915, he was joined by a very remarkable man, the famous Russian philosopher and writer P.D. Ouspensky, who became his pupil and took an active part in the organization of his work. I need not speak in detail of the years between 1915 and 1920. Ouspensky's own book, *In Search Of The Miraculous*,[1] gives a dramatic account of that period when Tsarist Russia was destroyed forever. A small, but devoted, circle of his Russian pupils continued their work with Gurdjieff to preserve for the world, through that time of chaos, what he himself had learned.

In 1918, he withdrew to the Northern Caucasus and

[1] *In Search Of The Miraculous.* Harcourt, Brace & Co., 1949.

undertook intensive practical teaching with a number of pupils who had succeeded in following him from Moscow and St. Petersburg. Civil war soon made life there impossible, and he undertook a hazardous journey through uninhabited regions of the Caucasus mountains and finally reached Tiflis, the capital of Georgia. The then government of Georgia was favorable to his work, and gave him facilities for re-establishing his Institute in Tiflis. Here, new pupils came to him of diverse nationalities. He began to elaborate his teaching of the sacred dances and rhythmical exercises which he had studied in Central Asia and the Far East. He had long before gained in Asia the reputation of being the greatest living authority on temple dances, some of which he had studied in monasteries and temples difficult of access, where they were used for developing the spiritual powers of man.

In 1920, the tide of war and revolution flooded the Southern Caucasus. With great difficulty, Gurdjieff extricated himself and many of his pupils. He came to Constantinople, where I met him for the first time.

My first meeting with Gurdjieff was in the Palace of Kuru Chesme, the home of the Prince Sabaheddin, nephew of the Turkish Sultan, himself a profound student, who had told me that I was to meet the most remarkable man he had ever known. My first impressions of Gurdjieff were of the purity of his Turkish accent, rare for a Greek, and of his extraordinary knowledge of hypnotism, in which Sabaheddin and I were at that time greatly interested. His appearance was so striking that, for many years, I

An Introduction to Gurdjieff

did not realize that he was of only moderate stature. When he took off the kalpak he was wearing, his magnificient head, completely shaven, produced a strange sense of harmony with sweeping black moustaches, strong eyebrows and eyes which at first seemed jet black. When he smiled his whole appearance changed—even his eyes became light and transparent. I could not help feeling that I had met someone out of the ordinary run of men.

I learned that Ouspensky was independently giving lectures in Constantinople. Thomas de Hartmann, the Russian composer, who had been working with Gurdjieff on the music for his dances, and Alexander de Salzmann, the famous stage designer, had begun to develop their own particular lines as part of his general plan. Gurdjieff evidently did not intend to settle permanently in Constantinople, and asked me to help him to get to Europe.

In the meantime, Ouspensky's book, *Tertium Organum*,[1] had appeared in England and America, where it attracted considerable attention. Lady Rothermere had taken a keen interest in Ouspensky and a succession of telegrams arrived inviting him to London. Ouspensky decided to go to London alone. Gurdjieff remained some time longer in Turkey. He finally went to Berlin, preferring it to Western Europe because he always hoped to re-open the path to Russia where many of his pupils had remained.

Conditions in Germany made work there impossible, and in the autumn of 1922, he finally settled in France. He bought the Château du Prieuré at

[1] *Tertium Organum*, Alfred Knopf, Inc., New York, 1922.

Gurdjieff—The Man and His Work

Fontainebleau, and again started the Institute for the Harmonious Development of Man, with a nucleus of his older pupils from Tiflis and Constantinople. Many English people came to the Institute—either permanently or as visitors—mostly pupils of Ouspensky who, since the end of 1921, had been lecturing in London on Gurdjieff's system.

Very intensive work began. Gurdjieff planned demonstrations of his dances and exercises in Europe and the United States. His considerable material resources, accumulated before the war, had been dissipated in the course of travels made under such difficult and arduous conditions. It was indeed only possible to keep the Institute going because all those living at the Prieuré were prepared to work without respite on the farm and in the house on very meager rations. These very circumstances were converted by Gurdjieff into conditions for inner work and no one who spent even a week or two at the Prieure between 1922 and 1924 can forget the intensity of that particular period.

For me personally, my stay at the Prieure in the summer of 1923 was the start of a new life. From personal experience, I became convinced that what I had so far regarded as theoretically possible for man, could be realized in practice for myself, if I were prepared to work.

I was more than ever impressed by Gurdjieff's amazing versatility. While I was there, he was building a Russian steam bath, quarried out of the Fontainebleau rocks. No one could handle pickaxe and crowbar as he could. He was equally at home with the animals or repairing the power plant. He was a marvelous cook. But it was, above all, in the 'Study House', a building of unusual design, improvised from an astonishing variety of materials, that we saw the most striking demonstration of his powers. It was there that he worked out all the new and complicated dances which he was then teaching, showing each executant exactly how the movements should be made.

The theoretical explanations of cosmological and psychological questions—the development of the rich symbolism described in Ouspensky's *In Search Of The Miraculous*—gave place at this time to a severely practical approach, in which physical efforts played a large part. This, of course, had already started in the Caucasus, but there was now a new element—the germ of an objective which was beginning to take shape in our minds—the task to be accomplished of making his teaching known to the world.

His own time was divided between earning money and driving forward the work of the Institute. Finding himself in a strange country whose language even was quite unfamiliar, he could not engage in commerce with the same ease as in Russia or the Caucasus. He was thus thrown back on his knowledge of medicine and psychology. He undertook the cure of drug addicts and drunkards. By this most difficult and exhausting work—for which he had already long before been famous in Central Asia—he was able to earn the money required to keep the Institute going. I have myself seen the seemingly impossible cases he undertook and the almost miraculous results

achieved. But the strain on his physique was too great
and debts were accumulating, so he decided to go to
America before completing his preparations.

He went in 1925, taking with him some forty people
to give demonstrations of Sacred Dances and Movements, to give lectures and to meet a number of
important Americans who had expressed the wish to
know more of his Ideas. The visit, which only lasted
six weeks, was a success. He planned to return again in
the fall and found, in the United States and other
countries, branches of the main Institute in France.
He left behind a well-known English journalist, A.R.
Orage, the Editor of the *New Age* and the *New
English Weekly*, who made himself responsible for the
preparatory work.

Ouspensky had separated from him in 1925 and was
teaching in London in isolation from the other groups
of Gurdjieff's pupils. In this again, I think we must see
an example of Gurdjieff's experimentation and testing.
He more than once brought about a separation
between himself and his most valued pupils—perhaps
in order to see for himself how his ideas would affect
the lives of people out of contact with his personal
teaching.

Within a few weeks of Gurdjieff's return from
America, he was all but killed in an automobile
accident, as a result of which he lost his memory for
months, and only very gradually recovered. From a
profoundly moving passage written by him about that
time, we know of his realization that there was then
only a limited time available for the accomplishment
of his task. He resolved to put his ideas into the form of a

An Introduction to Gurdjieff

written exposition, so composed as to lead people step by step to an understanding of practical work upon themselves. The next ten years were entirely devoted to writing and he withdrew wholly from contact with the outside world, except for necessary business matters.

It is indispensable to refer to the general course of Gurdjieff's life during this period. While writing, he displayed an intensity of concentration that at times completely isolated him from his surroundings. Sometimes, he worked continuously day and night at the Prieuré. At others, he travelled, usually by car, in France and other European countries. Then he would often stop his car by the side of the road and write for hours on a stone or in a wayside café. Much of his work was done at the Café de la Paix in Paris, where, amidst the bustle and confusion of the life around him, he would write all day and late into the night. No one could speak to him, however urgent the occasion, until he turned his attention to them of his own accord.

He wrote mostly in Russian. The manuscript was translated into English, French and German, each version being constantly re-read to him for correction. Those who participated in this work have described it as unlike any ordinary experience.

In order to have even an approximate conception of the work undertaken by Gurdjieff between 1927 and 1948, it would be necessary to read and study the Third Series of his writings, which have been only accessible to students who have already worked on the First and Second Series. His work was partly concerned with his own inner world, partly with the needs of his worn-out body, and partly with the, what he calls, "obscure but all-important factors in the human psyche." It is this latter motive which is hard to understand for anyone who imagines that the modern European or American is a normal, *balanced* human being. On the contrary, all, with few exceptions, are unbalanced people who have quite lost contact with reality and whom, therefore, it is very difficult to help towards a normal sane existence.

Gurdjieff came more and more clearly to see that the ways of helping people which have been used in the past are no longer applicable—because modern man cannot even listen to what is most necessary for him to hear. Notwithstanding so many years of profound study of the human psyche, Gurdjieff reached the conclusion, as late as 1927, that a new and more penetrating approach to the problem must be undertaken. He accordingly imposed on himself a way of life that would, as he says, "cause each person to take off the mask kindly provided by their papa and mama," and disclose the depths of his or her nature. The procedure adopted he describes as "finding the most sensitive corn of each person from whatever class or race he might come and whatever position he might hold, and treading on it rather violently." It can well be imagined that such procedure made him many new enemies and even scandalized many old friends. Since he carried his procedure into every kind of relationship, it is not surprising that stories of a most damaging nature should have begun to spread at his expense.

An Introduction to Gurdjieff

Very few people were able to see the necessity or even the sense of his actions and there is no question that many obstacles were created to the acceptance of his teaching. Nevertheless, for anyone who has felt the obscurity of the human psyche, it is obvious that what he did was indispensable—partly to establish the facts which it was necessary to know and partly, also, for the further aim—equally important and necessary—namely, to try and recover his own health. Not only was his bodily strength almost destroyed by the automobile accident, but he carried the results of many serious diseases contracted in the course of his travels in different parts of the world.

In 1931, he again visited New York and, before the outbreak of the Second World War, paid several further visits to America. The Prieuré was finally closed down in 1932, and in 1934 he settled in Paris. He was there when war broke out, and remained throughout the German occupation. In spite of all difficulties, he continued, and even started new work with his French pupils. He held them together, teaching them new methods appropriate to the conditions in which they were living. His manuscripts were constantly being read in his presence and revised, in order to bring to perfection the exposition of his ideas.

The period from 1939 to 1948 was one of the utmost difficulty and privation for himself and his work. Those who were directly in contact with him were fewer in number than in the past, while those who misunderstood his ideas and mistrusted his methods had increased. Very much misunderstanding existed.

Gurdjieff—The Man and His Work

Only a few who knew him well and had worked closely with him had some understanding of his aim. But the three Series of Writings had been prepared and were available when a propitious moment for their publication should arrive. They were being studied in manuscript form in various parts of the world by small groups of his former pupils. All was ready. The seeds sown during the previous fifty years had grown to maturity. Externally at its lowest ebb, his work had reached an inner intensity greater than ever before. Through what channels was this force to be released?

In 1948, he began to let it be known that the time had come for a new phase of work. He had completed, some time before this, the testing of the methods which he had worked out, proving their suitability for our abnormal conditions of life, and for the peculiar psyche of western people. He also judged that there would be a sufficient time before a fresh onset of tension in the world for these ideas to spread. If they were able to spread widely enough and rapidly enough, they might perhaps so change people's understanding that if such a state of tension again arises, the forces released should direct themselves into positive rather than destructive channels.

So it came about that in the summer of 1948, many people who had not seen each other for many years, and others who had never met at all, began to arrive in Paris and went round to see him in his little flat, re-establishing contact first with him and then with one another. Everything seemed to be going normally as if work with him would continue as before, when again there was one of these automobile accidents

An Introduction to Gurdjieff

which, with bullet wounds and disease, make a terrifying pattern in his life. Once again, by all ordinary standards, he should have been killed. My wife and I were with him in Paris at that time. He was driving down to Cannes and we were following him down the next day. He returned in an ambulance, and I had perhaps the most extraordinary experience of my life when I saw, with my own eyes, the power he had over his own body. He was terribly injured by this accident, which should have killed any man, let alone a man over seventy, but he very quickly recovered.

It seems to me that, in some way connected with this accident, a decision was taken that he could at last go forward with his plans for the dissemination of his Ideas. Soon after this accident, he took the decision that he would publish the First Series of his writings, and charged some of his older pupils to undertake the arrangements for printing. Four translations were taken to America, Great Britain, Germany and France. Translations into Russian and Spanish were to follow. Having selected the United States as the first country in which his books should appear, he made a private visit to New York in December 1948. He remained until the end of January, by which time he had completed the arrangements with Harcourt Brace and Company for the publication of his own book and also of Ouspensky's book, *In Search Of The Miraculous.*

He spent his seventy-second birthday in New York and I have a vivid memory of him surrounded by his old pupils with many of their children sitting at his feet. His moustaches were now white, but his head was still clean shaven, and his complexion as fresh as when I had first met him nearly thirty years before. His smile came more frequently, and conveyed an overwhelming compassion and goodness. To those of us who heard him speak to the pupils who came to see him from many parts of America, it was clear that a great step forward was being prepared.

He returned to Paris and intensified his work. Pupils began almost daily to arrive from France and other countries to visit him at his little flat in the center of Paris. Many hundreds received personal help and guidance from him in the course of the year. He simplified and concentrated his message ever more and more—*only by the unremitting struggle of the individual for his self-perfecting can a force be created which will change the world.*

Driving himself as always, unmercifully, he alarmed those of us who were in close touch with him, lest his physical strength should prove unequal to the demands he was making upon himself. He attached the utmost importance to the early appearance of his book in America and would himself have sailed to New York on October 20th to give it his final personal direction.

But the end came suddenly. He died in the American Hospital in Paris on October 29th. There his body lay for four days, visited by hundreds of his pupils, including many who had flown over from the United States, from England and other countries. His funeral was a moving demonstration of the love and trust which he had inspired in those who knew him. The Russian Cathedral in Paris was crowded. There were his own pupils from France and from countries overseas, side by side with hundreds of Parisians from every walk of life, who knew him as philanthropist and good friend of those in need of help. The funeral oration pronounced by the Russian Archimandrite was a noble tribute to a deeply religious man who had long ceased to be associated with any one church or any one creed.

Gurdjieff's teaching is in his writings. They are his final message to his fellow men. Those of us who have studied with him for many years are convinced that his teaching corresponds to the needs of a world which is passing through a momentous transition. We want, in these days above all, to learn how to live, to know both what we ought to do and also how to do it. This is what Gurdjieff has taught us. He leaves the scene at the moment when his work is done. His writings are far more than a fitting memorial of a great life: they are the material for a new world.

3

"WORK ON ONESELF"

3

"WORK ON ONESELF"

Through and through, Gurdjieff's teaching is practical. It is concerned with the concrete situation of our immediate existence and what we make of it. This is equally true whether it is on the scale of the momentary choice of 'yes' or 'no', or whether it shows us how to find our own answer to the ultimate question: 'what is my significance in the Universe?' But, because we are so subjective and so full of illusion, we cannot even begin to understand concrete reality either within ourselves or outside, without preparation. We cannot even come to the idea of "work on ourselves" without preparation. Gurdjieff cannot speak to people with no sense of reality—only to those who already have some degree of understanding. Therefore, before I can begin to describe his methods of work, I must say something about preparation.

The first task is the clarification of one's own aim. This everyone has to do for himself. I cannot borrow or steal an aim from someone else. I have to decide for myself what is my aim. My aim is not what I ought to want or what I think I want, or what is popularly held or unpopularly held to be a worthy object in life, but

An Introduction to Gurdjieff

what in fact I do want more than anything else. I have to ask myself, if I embark on what is bound to be difficult work—that is to become something which I am not, to raise myself to a higher level of existence—am I prepared to pay the price? Is this aim to me more important than fame, riches, or the appreciation and admiration of my fellow men, or my own comfort or security, or my bodily desires and needs, or all the other things I may value. Are these more important than my own being? This is simple, commonsense thinking which everyone must undertake for himself, and moreover he must try, as far as he can, to be honest about it, realizing always that if we aim at something supremely valuable, we cannot expect it to be cheap.

The second preparatory task is to try, as far as we can, to take stock of our present situation. The first is to decide what I want; the second is to decide what I have or what I am. We can do this to a limited extent even with the few preliminary ideas that we may have, providing we understand one principle which is the necessity to distinguish between real and imaginary; to admit that only what is concrete and verifiable must be accepted as a starting point.

I can see for myself whether I am able to control my own inner states or my external manifestations. I must know whether I can answer the questions most vital to me. I can look at the sufferings of the world—individual and collective—and ask myself whether I have the knowledge or the power to relieve it. I can survey my own future and see before me old age, infirmity and death—and try to penetrate the mystery of life and its meaning and, in doing so, realize my own ignorance and helplessness. From this, I can turn to the possibility of new knowledge which may perhaps show me the way out and then ask myself once again—*what is such knowledge worth to me?*

This brings us to the third task, when we are confronted with the hope of finding at least something on which we can rely. Our next duty is clear. It is to verify, as far as we can, whether or not this new factor corresponds to our own needs and our own understanding. No one else can take this responsibility for us, and we have no right to expect that anyone else, whether an individual or an organization, should do so. If I am lost in a forest, and somebody claims to show me the way out, I alone must take the responsibility of deciding whether to follow his suggestions or to continue trying on my own, and I shall be wise if I verify as far as possible whether or not he knows anything about the forest or about orientating himself, whether or not he possesses a compass and a map. If I do not do these things but blindly trust myself to him, and subsequently find myself more lost than before, this is my responsibility, and I must reap the consequences of it.

These are elementary, commonsense principles, which everyone can and must apply for themselves as far as this is in their power, before they embark on a way that is new and untried. And what I am going to discuss now, must seem a most hazardous undertaking—the application of methods which you have so far not tested and tried, for the attainment of an aim you have not yet truly clarified, and which in any case is

An Introduction to Gurdjieff

almost impossible to describe.

One can, it is true, find various more or less satisfying verbal formulations: to change our level of *being;* to attain to life in a world different from the ordinary world of mechanical happenings; to become *real* men and women instead of machines or semi–animals, such as we and all people are. But we must realize that, however we may formulate the aim, the implied change in ourselves is so fundamental that we cannot tell its nature in advance. If we have taken these three preliminary questions seriously—we have decided that, such as we are, we know no way out of life, and no way out of death, and that to find the way out must be more important to us than turning round and round in this squirrel's cage in which we live—then we have surely come to the point of being prepared, at least to experiment with, and to see if we can verify, methods which claim not merely to show us the way out but enable us to take it.

So we come to the position where we are ready to talk about "how." In the heading of this lecture I put the words "work on oneself" in quotation marks. I write it so, because I am used to people saying, "What does this mean?" and professing to be unable to understand how "work on oneself" differs from ordinary attempts to live an upright life. Such people see nothing special in the idea. Others put forward theories about the impossibility of doing anything about oneself, because this would imply an inner division.

I can remember how long it took me personally to understand what is meant by "work on oneself." I have

"Work on Oneself"

noticed that Ouspensky refers to a similar difficulty in his first contact with Gurdjieff's teaching. A passage at the beginning of *In Search Of The Miraculous* describes his first meeting with one of Gurdjieff's groups in Moscow, and he says:

> When I asked what was the system they were studying and what were its distinguishing features, I was answered very indefinitely. Then they spoke of "work on oneself," but in what this work consisted they failed to explain.

* * *

At this point during the original exposition of the Lecture, Mr. Bennett conducted the following experiment:

"I have been thinking how I can try to convey to you what is meant by 'work on oneself'. It occurred to me to suggest that you should make a simple experiment with me, which might help you to make clear one or two things that I want to explain to you this evening. I want each one of you to hold your arms straight above your head."

Mr. Bennett then held his own arms straight above his head and everyone in the hall (there were about 350 people present) did the same. After a few seconds he said:

"Now stretch your arms as far as you can."

An Introduction to Gurdjieff

All the arms then went up by anything up to four inches. Mr. Bennett then asked those present to count one, two, three, four; four, three, two, one; two, three, four, five; five, four, three, two; three, four, five, six; and so on. When they had reached twelve, he asked them to stretch their arms again. It was at once obvious that nearly everyone had allowed their arms to drop. Mr. Bennett then continued:

"What do you notice? That when your attention had been taken away from your arms by putting it to the counting, you relaxed the effort to straighten them, and when I said, 'straighten your arms again,' almost all the arms, without exception, went up an inch or two.

"I want to use this to illustrate what I mean by 'work on oneself'. In the first place, to put your arms above your head was perhaps to some people an effort, because they thought this was a ridiculous thing to do in a lecture hall. But nearly everyone made this effort whether they thought it ridiculous or not. Then came an illustration of the relation of our will to our own body. You put your arms above your heads but—with very few exceptions, and those mostly people who had done it before—you did not make a special effort to straighten them. It was only when I drew

82

"Work on Oneself"

attention to it and said, 'stretch your arms,'
that you realized there was an additional
effort to be made. So long as you were
making this additional effort, most people's
arms continued to be straight, but only until
we began to count. Then the effort was
diverted from the stretching of your arms to
the counting, and the unusual way of
counting engaged your attention so that you
no longer made the effort of stretching your
arms. At the end when I said, 'stretch your
arms,' almost all arms straightened and went
up an inch or two. Two factors are involved
in this. One is the ability and decision to
make a certain effort, and the second is the
work of attention. Even if I decide to make a
certain effort, I can only continue so long as
a sufficient quantity of attention is available."

*   *   *

You will notice that I speak about attention as
though it were something material, and so it is.
Attention is matter; it is a particular kind of energy or
material of which, at any given moment, we have a
certain quantity in our organism. When that certain
quantity is used up (if we use it faster than we produce
it), we cannot, whatever decision we may make,
whatever necessity there may be, continue to control
our attention. This is generally true of everything we
do—all inner and outer processes in the life of man
depend upon matter or energy. If we have the

necessary material or energy for a process, that process is possible.

Energy is of different kinds. All matter is not of the same kind as wood or coal, which, when burned, releases its energy merely in the form of heat. Some energy is of a higher kind, more versatile, such as electrical energy. Other energy is connected with excited states of matter. Then there are still higher forms of energy, that go beyond the possibility of detection with ordinary physical apparatus. Everyone who reads even popular books on physics knows that as the frequency of vibrations of radiant energy increases, when the number per second reaches something like one with twenty zeros after it, it scarcely can be perceived at all; it passes through matter, through all the earth's atmosphere, and can hardly be detected. If it had twenty–two zeros, it would probably pass through quite undetected and we should have no means of knowing that such energy exists. There are very good reasons for presuming that there are still higher forms of energy which are not detectable by those types of electrical apparatus which we use today, and which, after all, we have only used in relatively recent years. Such energy is connected with experience, with thoughts, with feelings, with sensations and so on. Just as the energy of ordinary thought processes and sensations is a step above the radiant energy that we can detect with our apparatus, the energy with which we have the power of controlling our attention is one step higher than the energy of thoughts, feelings and sensations. And higher than this is still another form of energy that

"Work on Oneself"

plays a vital part in the life of man. This is the energy which enables us to make decisions, to choose. It is not by the power of thought, by the power of sensation, that we can choose. It is not even with the energy of attention. It is one step higher removed up the scale.

Now, you will ask: how is this discussion of the different kinds of energy relevant to the problem of self-creation, of *working on ourselves?* Work on ourselves has, at least as one of its primary purposes, the production in our organism of these higher forms of energy, which in the first place enable us to choose and take real decisions. These higher forms of energy are also able to transform our own functions, thinking, feeling and the rest, and raise them to a higher level. Finally, they can form something in us by which we can live entirely in a different world from the ordinary mechanical world of every day life.

Before I continue to discuss the work of energy, I shall discuss the psychology of man in as simple terms as possible. We have three primary groups of functions— *thinking, feeling* and *sensing.* They work with different parts of our nervous system, using nervous energy which is connected with electrical discharges, and they have the limitations corresponding to this kind of energy. They are no more than very complicated electrical machines, not so very different from those that mathematicians and physicists are constructing in their laboratories. One of these machines thinks, another feels, while the third is engaged in the activity of the body. The first is connected with the work of the cerebral hemispheres.

An Introduction to Gurdjieff

It is what we usually call our "brain." The second is connected with the sympathetic nervous system, the main center of which is in the solar plexus, and with the other ganglia associated with it. The third is based upon the spinal chord, and certain regions in the head. If this were all that existed or could exist in man, he would be no more than a collection of machines—very complicated and able to do very wonderful work—but still no more than machines. But we know that we have some kind of experience or awareness and we know that there is such a thing as attention. What are they ? Where do they come from?

The energy with which these three machines usually work is too low in the scale to which I referred to carry with it what we call "experience," that is inner awareness of a process as part of the process itself. For example, you can easily see that your nervous system is constantly receiving impressions from outside—but you are seldom aware of them. If your clothes are comfortable, you do not notice their touch on your body. There are many sounds all the time that you do not hear. There are thoughts in your mind that you do not notice, feelings which affect your awareness only indirectly. All this constant activity of your three brains can go on—and for the most part does go on—without any experiencing on your part; that is without any part of you being *aware* of it.

At the same time, experience is possible: it is indeed the only part of our life which is of any immediate importance to us. Experience depends on a higher grade of energy than simple nervous activity. Controlled attention requires a higher grade still. Most of

"Work on Oneself"

us will sit on a chair and not be aware of the pressure of our bodies on the seat, but if we bring our attention to it, we quickly become aware of it. People do not realize how very little they are aware of what goes on even in their thinking brains, and nearly all that goes on in their feeling brain is what we call unconscious, not associated with attention. At the same time, these three brains are the whole of our mechanism of response to our environment. It is with them that we live. What we call our conscious experience is mainly associated with our thinking brain, and what is commonly called the unconscious or sub-conscious is mainly associated with the feeling or sensing parts. This division is quite artificial. We can be quite conscious with these other parts, and we do not realize how little we are conscious of our thinking part. There are certain simple experiments that can be made that will demonstrate to anyone that they are not aware of the thoughts that go on in their thinking brain.

This is the first picture of man. He has three brains, three nervous machines with which he can experience because there is in him the energy of attention. So long as his energy of attention is not controlled from within, his experience is quite automatic and passive. What attracts his attention, he experiences; he is not his own master, but the slave of whatever happens to catch and hold his attention. His experience depends on the accidental activity of his nervous system.

When he begins to control and direct his attention, then to some extent he experiences what he wants to experience. For example, if I direct my attention towards my thoughts, I can think what I decide to think and not what happens to come into my mind, but if I do not make this effort of attention, my thoughts can be only automatic associations, verbal associations and so on, and what I will be thinking a minute hence is quite unpredictable. That is the ordinary state of the working of the thinking brain. It is by attention that intentional experience comes, that control, and therefore change, becomes possible. But attention alone does not give freedom. Attention alone is not the same thing as will. What we ordinarily call "will" is merely the resultant of all the forces that work on our attention and pull us this way and that way. *Real will* is connected with the higher energy about which I spoke, in which there is the power of *effective decision*. This implies, at the very least, full power over our own organism. It implies much else besides, but for the moment I am concerned with the primary necessity, that my "I" should have power over my thoughts, feelings, sensations and my bodily reactions in general. For ordinary people the impulse for their thoughts, feelings and bodies comes from their desires, their attractions and aversions. These are of course held within the limits imposed by training and habit; but, so far as the setting in motion or activation of all these bodily and psychic processes are concerned, the active principles are the forces of desire and aversion, attraction and repulsion. In so far as *these* control us, *we* control nothing, for they arise without our will or intention.

Now let me try to sort out this rough sketch I have been giving you. The first picture is of man as a being who has three mechanisms for living, three mech-

"Work on Oneself"

anisms for response to the external world,—thinking, feeling, sensing.

The work of the three brains can be quite automatic, without any intention or purpose, or it can be controlled either through the direction of attention, or in a still higher way through the presence of something which is independent of both the brains and the attention. I have thus made, in two ways, a threefold division of man. The first is a division of man into three parts, as far as mechanical functions are concerned, and the second is into three parts, as far as his possible level of experience is concerned. Such a classification is sufficient to explain the methods of work, but I must say at once that it is very much simplified and, when you come to study it in detail, many adjustments and corrections will have to be made. I am at this stage only using a first approximation to enable me to introduce these ideas to you.

The next question that we have to ask now is where, in this, am I? What is *myself* in all this? Is myself either the whole or part of my thinking brain? Is myself my feelings, my emotional states, my likes and dislikes? Or is myself my body, and all the experience of my body—that is, what I call the sensing brain or sensing mechanism? If you will take the trouble to study and verify what I have been saying, you will see that these three brains nearly always work out of contact with one another, and are unaware of one another, so that if this self is in one brain, then it is not in another. This is one of the easiest things to verify. It thus quickly becomes clear that we cannot say "I am my thoughts," "I am my feelings," or "I am my body," and

An Introduction to Gurdjieff

yet I talk about myself as "I." This either implies that there is something in me that is separate from, and over and above, my thoughts, feelings and sensations, or else that I am talking about something which does not exist.

My "I" is my will. It is my existence as a free being. It is that which redeems me from the emptiness of a mere machine. But I have no "I"—my experience is a mere succession of accidental states induced by external shocks. Gurdjieff compares man to a taxi, whom any fare can pick up and drive wherever he pleases. A man with a real "I" is like a car with an owner, who is always one and the same. We have to saturate ourselves with the realization of this distinction.

I am not a machine because my brains are mechanical, but because I have no "I" to control and direct my brains. Of course, we know that a philosopher once said, "I think therefore I am." But the truth is that "I" do not think—"it thinks" in me. My experience of the thinking (or feeling or sensing for that matter) that goes on in me is something accidental and uncontrolled.

Because of this, there is nothing in me which can take decisions in any real sense of the term. Thoughts about decisions or feelings about decisions may arise in me: but by the time that action has to be taken, I may have no awareness at all of the present or no memory of the past. Only he who can say I am today, yesterday and tomorrow—the same one and indivisible—can be said to have an "I". When we begin to make an honest survey of the situation we are forced to admit that no such "I" exists in us. We cannot even picture to ourselves what such an "I" could be.

If there is not the "I" in me which should exist in a man worthy of the name—*why* is it absent? How should it have arisen? Gurdjieff answers: "In childhood, during the period of preparation for responsible age." We are taxis because our machine was never put into the hands of its real owner. The very thing which is the most necessary and essential part of a person, *that he should be capable of taking responsible decisions,* is absent even from people who most appear to have it, and pride themselves on having it. They confuse the automatic working of their three brains which comes from training and habit, with *real will,* with the real power of independent decision.

Why do both philosophers and also ordinary people talk about man and about themselves as if they had an "I"? Why do they believe in something which, according to what I have been saying, does not exist? The answer is that they want to believe it and therefore they call whatever experience happens to be present by the name of "I" even if it is quite unconnected with what was there a minute before, and even if it will change into something quite different a minute later. All this is called by Gurdjieff the "Imaginary I" in man, and he calls a man who has no real "I" a "man in quotation marks" and not a real man at all.

No doubt, you will have found it hard to accept and perhaps even to understand what I have been saying. That does not matter for the moment. I only wanted to introduce two or three ideas, which are necessary

An Introduction to Gurdjieff

for the subject matter of this lecture. I had to say something about the three brains, and about the distinction between the real and the illusory self, because practical methods are concerned with harmonizing and balancing these three brains so that they can work together, not separately, and with the discarding of the illusory or false self and the finding or formation of an "I", a real self.

The picture of a real man is that of a being who has an "I" that is an unchanging center of decision in himself; which can take decisions which are valid not only for this moment, but for tomorrow, next year, for the rest of his life if necessary; and which moreover is able to take decisions not only for one brain but for all three—whereas people like ourselves can do no more than take decisions that affect one of our brains at a time. Now how is a man to have such an "I" if it cannot exist in one of the brains without putting that brain out of balance with the rest? Evidently, he must have something in him which exists, which holds together, apart from his own nervous system—apart even from his own bodily organism.

This brings us to an idea which is very ancient, but which has taken so many distorted forms that we must try to formulate it clearly; that is the idea of the *higher bodies* of man. Every kind of theory about higher bodies in man has been put forward—that man has astral, mental, causal or many other bodies; or that he can have a second body, the "Resurrection Body" of the Pauline Epistles. Sometimes, instead of the word body, such words as "soul" or "spirit" are used. But in every case, they imply something which is not of the

92

"Work on Oneself"

same stuff as the physical body.

Whatever name may be given to this "something" which is the seat of the real man—of his "I"—people agree that he either has it and that all men have it, or that it is a mere fiction and does not exist in anyone. Gurdjieff does not teach either the one or the other. He says we *can* have higher bodies or souls—but in order to have them they must be created by our own work. He teaches that man is born and lives, so far as the ordinary mechanical level of existence is concerned, with only one body—the ordinary physical body, obeying physical and mechanical laws. That body, like every other material object, is subject to decay in time, and at death disintegrates and disappears and has no further unified existence. At the same time, man can form in himself a second body, which is made of a higher order of matter than his physical body. It is, in fact, just through this body —when it exists—that unified instead of dispersed experience is possible. The attention of a man without the second body can never separate itself from his three brains and stand apart from them. It is the second body which can have true voluntary attention, real power over thoughts, feelings and bodily experience.

This second body is formed in man as a result of a certain kind of struggle which I am going to discuss. In those who have it, its existence can be verified not only by psychological, but even by physical tests. When the physical body dies, then, because it is not made of the same material, the second body does not disintegrate. At the same time, it is not the vehicle of

93

the true self, the independent will. These belong to the third body in man. This is made from the highest form of energy, which—to avoid going into very long descriptions connecting it in your minds with misleading associations—I call the energy of will, or energy of decision. When the third body is formed, a man becomes in the full sense of the word a free being. He has complete power over himself. He can exist without dependence on the first or physical body. The third body is the seat of the will, and without the third body, there can only be evanescent, transitory will; there cannot be any permanent will in man. The third body is the soul in the Christian sense. It is the "wedding garment" of the parable. It is of the third body that Christ speaks when He says "What shall it profit a man if he gain the whole world and lose his own soul?"

You may remember that in the first lecture I spoke about two different destinies for man—either he can have the destiny of animals, on the deterministic level, or he can raise himself to a second level in which not only his own existence is different, but in which his relations with other people are also different. This is a simplification, because there is more than one level possible, but roughly speaking, we can say that the man who has the second body actually exists in a different world from the man who has only a first body, and the man with a third body exists in a different world and has a different present and a different future from the man who only exists in two, or in the one body. Fully balanced normal existence for man is the existence in which he has three bodies,

and independent experiences in each of the three
bodies. This is attainable, not by a change of
experience alone, but by a chemical process. Let me
explain why I call it a "chemical process." The chemist
takes certain materials, lets them act on one another
under approximate conditions and obtains other
compounds which are more valuable, the whole
process being subject to natural quantitative laws.
There is always a certain price to be paid for what he
does—he either has to put energy into the process, or
he has to discard something in the course of getting
what he wants.

It is exactly this which is involved in the process of
creation of our own being. A man is like a chemical
factory. He takes in three different kinds of raw
material: the food we eat, the air we breathe and the
impressions that come into us through our sense
organs. These are all sources of energy. We are
familiar with the idea that our food is transformed into
energy in our bodies. The air we breathe not only
takes part in the simple process of producing heat
energy, but in more complicated chemical processes it
builds up substances necessary for our life and for
these higher energies about which I have spoken.
Every time that a nerve ending is stimulated by light,
heat, touch or whatever it may be, a corresponding
energy enters my body and there is a nervous
discharge.

Ordinary people make no use at all of the
possibilities of their chemical factory and even destroy
its products. They are like a very unproductive,
wasteful factory that employs thousands of operatives

An Introduction to Gurdjieff

and manages to do no more than to keep the factory itself supplied with raw material, with nothing to sell and nothing to store. They use up all the energy they produce without gaining anything at all either for themselves or for any higher purpose, or for the good of their neighbours.

If we wish to increase the output of this human chemical factory, we must work on two things. There are two main departments where the working of the factory can be changed. The first is the department of *attention.* The alchemists who used their own terminology to describe various psychological things (the word alchemy means "psychological transformation" in man) used the word "quicksilver" and they used to say one has to "learn to fix one's quicksilver." We have to learn how to bring this very wayward energy of attention, so subtle and so hard to hold, under control. If we do this, certain changes take place in the inner working of our organism. When I direct and hold my attention, a transformation of energy takes place, which produces material that can be used for various purposes. First of all, energy is used up in my psychic activity and in the life of my body. Secondly, I am constantly radiating energy out into space. This energy is not wasted, but is needed for the general purposes of life. If I make the effort to control my attention, the quality of my radiation changes and this has an important result about which Gurdjieff has much to say in his writings. Then there is the third use of energy of attention, which is for the formation and growth of my higher bodies.

The second department in the chemical factory,

whose work must be made more effective, deals with even stronger forces than the power of attention. I am only going to speak about one aspect of this energy; that is the force of sacrifice or suffering. In suffering, there is a transformation of energy of a higher order. If I am the slave of my own egoism, then the energy liberated by suffering will go into some such process as self-pity, worry, fear, anger, irritation, indignation, jealousy, envy, and be quite wasted as far as I am concerned. Now this energy happens to be of very special value; it is one of the foods of my own higher body. Whether I wish it or not, I must produce this energy; that is, I must suffer. But it is in my own hands to make this suffering useful. If I do not do so, it is not merely wasted—it actually becomes a poison and can do me great harm, even in my ordinary mechanical existence. We all know how quickly men and women degenerate if once they give themselves up to suffering, whether it is of the type of self-pity and anxiety or whether it is violent in the form of anger and hatred. We have equally clear evidence of the positive results of suffering which is not allowed to flow into egoistic channels. The best and most beautiful characters we meet in our ordinary life are nearly always moulded by suffering rightly borne.

So far, I have spoken only of "involuntary suffering," that is suffering which comes without our choice or intention. This has only limited possibilities, for it can never be wholly conscious. Quite different results can be gained from what Gurdjieff calls "voluntary suffering."

There are certain changes which it is necessary for

me to bring about in myself which can only be obtained if I intentionally, of my own decision, put myself into a situation of suffering. I have many weaknesses, many defective processes, and the combination of those weaknesses and defects with my own imaginary self—my imaginary I, the picture I have of myself—brings me into a state of almost complete slavery. On the one hand I cannot overcome my weaknesses, and, on the other, I cannot give up my picture of myself as not weak. Between these two I am constrained to pretend to myself and to pretend to other people; to hide all the time what I really know to be present and to try to show what does not really exist; in short, to live a life of lies. In this condition, no liberation of the higher energy is possible, because whatever energy is developed will inevitably flow into the channels of jealousy, self–pity, irritation, anger and the rest. If I understand this, I see that there is nothing for it but to put myself into such a situation that this constraining channel of weakness on the one side and self–love on the other will be broken down. In doing so, not only shall I prevent this energy from being lost, but I shall actually bring about a more complete transformation—by which the building up of the material, needed for the higher body, can be accelerated sufficiently to achieve it within the time that is available to me.

This is the general conception of the process of self-creation in man. Gurdjieff calls it, "conscious labour and intentional suffering," and it runs like a golden thread throughout his writings. I have tried only to give you some idea of the meaning of this

"Work on Oneself"

phrase, of the kind of effort and work it implies.

I shall not say more about these general methods in these lectures, for they are only important when they are taken practically—and they can only be taken practically when they have been understood and the necessity for "work on oneself" has penetrated into one's very being. Before I conclude this lecture, I want to give you some account of special methods which occupy an important place in Gurdjieff's teaching. You will have already understood that work on attention and the effort to overcome the resistances of our own organism are necessary elements in "work on oneself." We also have to learn how to develop the powers latent in our three brains and bring them into harmony with one another. Gurdjieff studied particularly, and taught as a very important part of his whole work, methods for developing, harmonizing and unifying the three brains through physical work. These methods are called for convenience "Movements." They were brought together by Gurdjieff from many eastern and a few western schools which have studied the use of rhythmic movements and sacred dances, and they form a very important part of his teaching. As I have already stated, he was long known in Asia as the greatest authority on temple dancing. Perhaps some of you have seen demonstrations of his Movements. The Movements are one important and valuable feature of his teaching. They shorten considerably the work of studying, in the first instance, then of becoming conscious and of eventually being able to use the three brains rightly and in harmony. To help people to find and understand the

An Introduction to Gurdjieff

working of their feeling and sensing parts, use of a special kind of music is made. Gurdjieff made a very profound study of music, and the use of vibrations in general, and the part they play in human life.

Then, as regards the psychological study of man —that is the means by which one can study oneself and other people—he devised a detailed system of psychology which I will not speak about because you can read about it in Ouspensky's *In Search Of The Miraculous.*

Gurdjieff had certain other special methods of conveying that deeper knowledge which is too subtle to be put into ordinary verbal formulae. He made very great use of more than one special kind of symbolism. Some of these are described in Ouspensky's *In Search Of The Miraculous.* In his own book, in the First Series of his writings, he makes use of a number of different symbolisms, one within another, so that quite simple ideas are expressed; but the more deeply you study, the more subtle ideas you find within these. For teaching people in contact with him, he often used to employ a symbolism created on the spur of the moment for those who could understand it. Sometimes one might see thirty or forty people in the room, of whom each understood quite differently what he intended to tell them, because he would use a symbolism of a form that would evoke different responses in different people. In this way, there was a progression in his methods of teaching that corresponds to what he called three circles or three degrees. He calls these three the "exoteric," the "mesoteric" and the "esoteric," or the outer, middle and inner

"Work on Oneself"

circles. A person who comes in contact with his ideas and who, having answered for himself the three preliminary questions about which I spoke, has decided that he wishes to learn has entered the exoteric or outer circle. For those in this circle, a certain kind of knowledge and a certain kind of method are available. Those who satisfy themselves and also show by their life that this can give objectively the results they are seeking, pass into the second circle. This involves quite different demands and those in it can receive quite different help. One may say that in the first or exoteric circle, no demands are made, because no demands can be made of people who understand nothing and have no control over themselves. When people begin to understand and have a certain degree of control over themselves, and want more and are prepared to pay more, different kinds of relationship can be established. The third or inner circle is that in which the pupil comes to grips with reality. Once he enters it he must hold on to it until he achieves his aim.

The work which starts inside—at the root of my own nature—must by degrees find its way out. Firstly, into my dealings with those nearest to me. Next, into my relations with my fellow-men in general. Ultimately I may hope that it will lead me step by step to discover and realize the sense of my existence and bring me face to face with my Creator.

4

GURDJIEFF'S WRITINGS

4

GURDJIEFF'S WRITINGS

In the account of Gurdjieff's Life and Work which I gave in the Second Lecture, I said that he had composed three Series of Writings designed to lead the reader step-by-step to an understanding of what is meant by "work on oneself." At the end of the last lecture, I referred to his division of his pupils into three groups or circles, according to their degree of practical understanding of this work. It will, no doubt, have occurred to you that there must be some connection between these two sequences of three; and the word 'esoteric' may have conveyed to you the idea of something in his writings hidden from the profane, and revealed only to 'initiates'.

Before we begin to speak about Gurdjieff's writings, I want to say a little about his attitude to what is commonly called 'esotericism'.

We are used to hearing such words as 'esoteric' or 'occult' and they very easily lead to misunderstanding. They can be taken in quite a wrong way, as if to imply that some kind of important knowledge is deliberately hidden from people or that access to it is intentionally made more difficult than it need be; or, as if there were different kinds of knowledge, one kind of knowledge

An Introduction to Gurdjieff

reserved for special people and other kinds of knowledge which are inferior and open to everyone. These are quite wrong distinctions. Real knowledge, even the highest possible knowledge, is no more hidden from people than, let us say, the most advanced mathematics is hidden from people in a university. Anyone who wishes may go and hear the most abstruse lectures of which they cannot understand a single word, and this obviously brings no profit to them unless they are prepared to work through the preparatory stages. Until they are able to understand and use delicate subtle mathematical operations, it is quite useless for them to attend lectures by the great and famous teachers. There is no essential difference in the communication of knowledge connected with the destiny of man and the ultimate reality, except that it is not always so obvious that we do not understand what is being taught. If I were going to lecture on the calculus of tensors and you came in by mistake to see me writing a lot of symbols and formulae on the blackboard, those of you who were not specialists in the subject would realize that you had come to the wrong place and ask for your money back. But suppose someone were speaking about the really deep secrets of human nature; you would miss even more completely the real sense of what they were saying, but you would probably imagine you understood and so would give a quite wrong meaning to it. That would happen because the language in which they would speak about such things would necessarily be very subtle and elusive in order to convey the fine distinctions that are characteristic of ultimate reality.

Gurdjieff's Writings

Such fine distinctions cannot be expressed in the rough and ready formulae of our ordinary conversation. Conversations may take place in which very important and yet very subtle matters are discussed, and people may take a great deal of trouble and push themselves forward in order to be present at such conversations, thinking to gain something by it. It then usually happens that they not only miss the whole point of what is being said, but often understand something quite different, sometimes even dangerous to themselves.

Real knowledge has to be approached by stages, and especially real knowledge of an ultimate character. Gurdjieff described these stages in three very broad divisions, and I am going to speak about this first, before we come to his writings. *Real* knowledge can be conveyed from one person to another on three different levels. To these Gurdjieff gave the names "philosophical," "theoretical" and "practical."

The first and lowest of these is the *philosophical level.* Truth on this level can be conveyed only in terms of general principles, as a way of understanding. It does not approach the complexity and subtlety of actual facts and actual experience.

On the second or *theoretical level,* fundamental laws can be taught and learned. Once these laws are understood, it is possible to use them to solve particular problems. This is a great step forward from the first or philosophical stage. I do not mean that knowledge on the philosophical level has no value in practical life, but it only has value as a general guide, and many of the concrete problems which arise in actual life are not at all soluble in philosophical terms. Too many factors are involved. The problem is too small in relation to the greatness of the whole.

It is only on the *practical level* that everything becomes concrete. Here every individual can see himself as he really is, and his position in relation to others, and to the universe as a whole. Problems can be solved in such a way that there is no distinction between knowing and doing. There is not the distinction that we commonly draw between knowing what we should do and knowing how to do it.

The universe is very large and subject to laws of different grades. These laws interpenetrate and pass from one level to another. They become very complicated indeed by the time anything so small as individual man is reached. The complexity of the laws operating in the life of one individual man or woman is so great that often no solution of the practical problems of life can be found in philosophical or theoretical terms. It is only on a very advanced level that the problems of the individual can be seen in a concrete setting. This is quite contrary to our ordinary way of thinking. We imagine that the problems of individuals are within the compass of our understanding. We may even think it more difficult to understand great laws than to understand one man. It is not so.

Gurdjieff constructed the written exposition of his teaching in a form which corresponds to this division of levels of understanding. He wrote three series of books, one which deals with general principles, one which deals with theory, and the third which deals with the actual practice of the transformation of man.

Gurdjieff's Writings

The First Series is not a treatise on philosophy in the sense in which we should ordinarily understand it. It is concerned, as philosophy should be, with the reconstruction of our thought; with furnishing people with "valid categories," as they are called, that are sound materials for thinking; and it is concerned, above all, with getting rid of all faulty material that obstructs our thinking. Our modern world is far from any real understanding of the sense and significance of human life, and still further, by a very long way, from any possibility of doing anything effective to bring human life into normal channels. The objective of the First Series is therefore necessarily more critical than constructive, more to get rid of false conceptions about man than to furnish material for a new world.

At the very beginning of the First Series of his writings, Gurdjieff sets out the objectives of each of the Three Series, which exist under the collective title, *All and Everything.* I am going to quote the text of the title page for you as an introduction to what I am going to say further:

All and Everything

FIRST SERIES: Three books under the title of *"An Objectively Impartial Criticism of the Life of Man,"* or, *"Beelzebub's Tales to His Grandson."*

SECOND SERIES: Three books under the common title of *"Meetings With Remarkable Men."*

THIRD SERIES: Four books under the common title of *"Life Is Real Only Then, When 'I Am.'"*

Gurdjieff's Writings

All written according to entirely new principles of logical reasoning and strictly directed towards the solution of the following three cardinal problems:

FIRST SERIES: To destroy, mercilessly, without any compromises whatsoever, in the mentation and feelings of the reader, the beliefs and views, by centuries rooted in him, about everything existing in the world.

SECOND SERIES: To acquaint the reader with the material required for a new creation and to prove the soundness and good quality of it.

THIRD SERIES: To assist the arising, in the mentation and in the feelings of the reader, of a veritable, nonfantastic representation not of that illusory world which he now perceives, but of the world existing in reality.

An Introduction to Gurdjieff

I shall start with the First Series: *"An Objectively Impartial Criticism of the Life of Man,"* or, as it will be convenient to call it, *"Beelzebub."* This is an extraordinary book in every sense of the word. Gurdjieff devoted immense effort and time to its writing and revision. It is a long book—more than a thousand pages of print, and every page is important. To those who have read and studied it deeply—and it is worth mentioning that many of Gurdjieff's pupils have read it from cover to cover twenty times or more—it is an inexhaustible source of new knowledge and inspiration.

The purpose of the book is to help the reader to divest himself of his humanistic, geocentric attitude towards the problems of the universe and arrive at an objective standpoint. This is commonly supposed to be the task of the philosophers and you might expect to find a closely reasoned book in which history, psychology and sociology are analysed on the basis of some philosophical principle. Many such books have been written and they have changed little or nothing in the life of man. Gurdjieff's book deals with historical, psychological and sociological questions, but not by way of analysis and discussion. He has chosen for his exposition the form of a narrative relating the experiences of a being from another planet who visits the earth and studies the life of mankind. It can be conceived as a vast allegory into which historical and scientific information of immense interest is introduced as well as theoretical and practical teaching about human psychology and "work on oneself." I shall try to give you some idea of the form and content of the book, but before doing so I must not fail to emphasize the difficulty of reading it.

In the first place, the language is unfamiliar. New words are introduced to convey ideas which are quite new to our modern thought, or to give a fresh turn to old ideas. At first, the unfamiliarity of these new words produces a disconcerting impression—but this soon wears off and for most readers ceases to be much of an obstacle. Far more difficult is the form of the narrative itself. Sometimes the stories are very simple and touching, at others they convey an exceedingly subtle and elusive teaching. The narrative is not continuous, the thread often being broken to insert and emphasize some special idea. Much is conveyed in the form of dramatic pictures or allegories. It is almost impossible to tell without very deep and persistent study what is meant to be taken literally, what allegorically, and what in the form of a special symbolism. Many of the formulations are so compressed that no one could understand them without reference to other passages. The most important and valuable teaching is often introduced by the way in a passage which at first glance seems a mere repetition of something which has been said before.

These are not the only difficulties in reading *Beelzebub*. The central ideas are themselves very hard to understand and accept. Even when all that is said on a given subject is pieced together and studied, there remains a quality which eludes any ordinary intellectual approach. Often I have seen highly educated people, with a wide reading in the subject discussed, completely nonplussed by a passage which

An Introduction to Gurdjieff

a simple person approaching the subject only from feeling and common sense immediately understands and accepts. *Beelzebub* is difficult, but not in the sense that the *Summa Theologia* or the *Critique of Pure Reason* are difficult. It requires no special education or training—but it does make a peculiar demand on the reader—that he should sincerely desire to know and that he should be prepared to feel and sense as well as to think. Whoever is prepared to persevere will gain from his reading of *Beelzebub* that change of attitude towards himself and his destiny which is the necessary condition for "work on oneself."

But the difficulties of *Beelzebub* are not only intellectual. There are obstacles of quite a different kind in the subject matter itself. From start to finish the book outrages any susceptibilities the reader may have. The scientist is contemptuous of the dogmatic assertions which appear inconsistent with the most firmly established scientific 'facts'. The historian is amused or irritated at the disregard for all accepted chronology and the claim, made throughout the book, that the true course of history has been on quite different lines from what is generally accepted. The philologist can make no sense of the linguistic usage, nor the anthropologist of the statements about races and the migrations of peoples. The artist is pilloried as a useless degenerate and all our modern art denounced as an altogether harmful factor in human life. Religious susceptibilities are wounded by accounts of the life and work of the Founders of the great religions which are quite contrary to current beliefs. Our Western notions of good taste are shocked

Gurdjieff's Writings

by the open discussion of problems of sex and human relationships generally. National susceptibilities are outraged by merciless satires upon the life and customs of the various countries of the world. Our ideas of literary style are set at nought. Finally, there runs through the book a note of arrogant superiority which is utterly offensive to our notions of 'good form'. It is safe to say that no reader, at a first perusal of the book, will reach the last page without having been shocked and outraged at some point.

All this is obviously deliberate and an essential part of the whole plan. It is fundamental for the very approach which Gurdjieff makes to the human problem of the present day, that mankind is completely astray and that there is nothing—literally nothing —in our science, art, philosophy, religion, in our political and social systems which is not tainted through and through with false notions about man, with egoism and self-deception. I can assure you from my own experience of hundreds of people, who have read *Beelzebub* with persistent attention, that it helps them towards an objective and impartial attitude towards man better than any amount of explanation or advice.

Before reading you some typical passages, I will try and give you a summary of the narrative portions of the book as a whole.

The hero of the story is Beelzebub, who is represented as an angel or devil who, in his youth, revolted against what he conceived to be an injustice in the universe. In consequence of this he was exiled from the Center of the Universe to a very remote

An Introduction to Gurdjieff

place, our solar system. He lived on the planet Mars, but from time to time, visited the earth. His first descent was at the time of Atlantis, twelve thousand years ago. From time to time through the great civilizations of Egypt, Tikliamish, Babylon and so on, to recent times, further visits are made.

Nearly the whole of the book consists of a narrative of Beelzebub's Six Descents upon the planet Earth. The tales are told to his grandson Hassein, whose upbringing he has taken under his care. Man and his history are used by Beelzebub as illustrative material to develop in Hassein the power of impartial reasoning and compassion for suffering.

Man is described as a "three-brained being," with a special kind of destiny (differing from the destiny of two or one brained beings—animals and invertebrates)—in that the possession of three brains gives the power of choice. With this comes the possibility of self-creation, of forming in oneself true imperishable individuality. It is taken for granted that such beings exist on many planets in the universe and that most, if not all of them, have reached a higher level of development than man.

Our Earth is presented as a particularly unfortunate planet, where, owing to accidental, unforeseen events connected with the formation of our moon, the development of organic life on the earth passed through a long unfavorable period. This lasted many thousands of years corresponding to most of what geologists call the "Quaternary Period," when man had already appeared, but when it was not yet possible for man to exercise his true function—that is, of a being capable of developing himself. Because of this unpropitious situation existing on the earth, it was necessary to protect man from the realization of what he was missing, to protect him from the knowledge that he was different from the animals, and yet was unable to enter into possession of that very thing which made him different. This 'spiritual sterilization', as it were, of the higher possibilities of man, is described by Beelzebub as the implanting in our remote ancestors of a special organ connected with part of the nervous system which prevented man from seeing things as they really are; which made him see his destiny only in terms of his animal existence, and although he had the third brain—the power of thought—to use that only for the purposes of the animal existence. This organ is called the "organ Kundabuffer"—a word of fantastic etymology taken partly from a Sanskrit word meaning coiled and also a snake. Kundabuffer is stated to have been removed from man by a process of breeding, at a time when the relations between the moon and the earth had been so stabilized that this 'spiritual sterilization' was no longer necessary.

However, owing to the long period of time, tens of thousands of years, during which this organ had been present in these remote ancestors of ours, certain consequences had become inherent and remained as a predisposition towards self-deception and the inability to see things as they really are. Although man was liberated, he failed to use his liberty in the right way. This may be conceived as a way of expressing the theological notion of the "Fall of Man." In consequence, Man lost the power to raise himself to the level of existence which he should occupy by his own essential nature, that is, the essential nature of a self-creating being. This is the general conception of man that Beelzebub puts before Hassein.

This unfortunate, tragical situation of mankind on the earth is further represented as having attracted the attention of the higher levels in the universe and even of our All-Merciful Creator. The Creator Himself has, from time to time, sent Messengers, Beings of a higher nature than man, Sons of God, who incarnate on the earth in human form. In this form, they endeavour to re-open for man the way to liberation from the consequences of his early failure. Many of the early chapters are devoted to accounts of different ways in which this task has been undertaken. Beelzebub himself is represented, not as being directly concerned in these great tasks, but as having been entrusted from time to time with special undertakings on the earth, as, for example, to combat the spread of animal sacrifice, which was both disastrous for man and contrary to the whole meaning of man's relation with the higher powers. A number of chapters are concerned with the various measures Beelzebub took: the lines he followed in India, Central Asia and elsewhere to try to put an end to animal sacrifices. This is represented as having happened thousands of years ago, when animal sacrifices had reached disastrous proprotions. Not only the killing of animals, but the killing of man is taken as a disastrous feature of human life and, indeed, as the greatest of evils on the earth. War is a most unnatural process, contrary to the nature of three-brained beings. Beelzebub is shown in the third book, studying and trying to understand how it is possible that man can fall into such states that war is possible. One of the final chapters deals with war and the causes and prevention of war, about which I said a little in the first of these lectures.

That is the general thread running through the book—of man as a being unfortunate in relation to the general conditions of life on the earth but compensated to a great extent for this misfortune by the intervention of beings sent from Above. In connection with the practical issues, there are a number of stories illustrating the impossibility of achieving right results by wrong methods, by violence, by mere external organizations in which the people concerned in the organization remain themselves unchanged. There is also one very beautiful and striking series of chapters describing the legendary being Ashiata Shiemash, who is described as born of the Sumerian race, before the rise of Babylon. He is represented as having, for a short period, inaugurated and maintained on the earth normal conditions among people, not by external organization, but by having brought home to people the necessity for self-efforts, for work on the creation of their own being.

I propose to quote for you one or two passages which would be illustrative of this First Series and I

An Introduction to Gurdjieff

have chosen a short passage from this very chapter. Ashiata Shiemash, who is represented as one of the beings incarnated from Above, perhaps five thousand years ago, is described by Beelzebub as having studied closely the human problem in order to decide by what means he could renew the realization of the necessity for man to struggle for his own self-perfection. He has examined the three Sacred Impulses in man from which this striving should come—Faith, Hope and Love. At the point where I shall begin to quote, he has been studying these and meditating on the results of his studies, and then he says, quoting a record that was supposed to have been made by Ashiata Shiemash himself and later found by Beelzebub and studied by him:

> "'These meditations of mine made it categorically clear to me, that all the genuine functions proper to men–beings, as they are proper to all the three-centered beings of our Great Universe, had already degenerated in their remote ancestors into other functions, namely, into functions included among the properties of the organ Kundabuffer which were very similar to the genuine sacred being-functions of Faith, Love, and Hope.
>
> "'And this degeneration occurred in all probability in consequence of the fact that when the organ Kundabuffer had been destroyed in these ancestors, and they had

also acquired in themselves factors for the genuine sacred being–impulses then, as the taste of many of the properties of the organ Kundabuffer still remained in them, these properties of the organ Kundabuffer which resembled these three sacred impulses became gradually mixed with the latter, with the result that there were crystallized in their psyche the factors for the impulses Faith, Love, and Hope, which although similar to the genuine, were nevertheless somehow or other quite distinct.

"'The contemporary three–centered beings here do at times believe, love, and hope with their Reason as well as with their feelings; but how they believe, how they love, and how they hope—ah, it is exactly in this that all the peculiarity of these three being –properties lies!

"'They also believe, but this sacred impulse in them does not function independently, as it does in general in all the three–centered beings existing on the various other planets of our Great Universe, upon which beings with the same possibilities breed; but it arises dependent upon some or other factors, which have been formed in their common presences, owing as always to the same consequences of the properties of the organ Kundabuffer—as for instance, the particular properties arising in them which they call "vanity," "self–love," "pride," "self –conceit," and so forth.

"'In consequence of this, the three-brained beings here are for the most part subject just to the perceptions and fixations in their presences of all sorts of "Sinkrpoosarams" or, as it is expressed here, they "believe–any–old–tale."

"'It is perfectly easy to convince beings of this planet of anything you like, provided only during their perceptions of these "fictions," there is evoked in them and there proceeds, either consciously from without, or automatically by itself, the functioning of one or another corresponding consequence of the properties of the organ Kundabuffer crystallized in them from among those that form what is called the "subjectivity" of the given being, as for instance: "self–love," "vanity," "pride," "swagger," "imagination," "bragging," "arrogance," and so on.

"'From the influence of such actions upon their degenerated Reason and on the degene-rated factors in their localizations, which factors actualize their being–sensations, not only is there crystallized a false conviction concerning the mentioned fictions, but the-reafter in all sincerity and faith, they will even vehemently prove to those around them, that it is just so and can in no way be otherwise.

"'In an equally abnormal form were data moulded in them for evoking the sacred impulse of love.

"'In the presences of the beings of contemporary times, there also arises and is present in them as much as you please of that strange impulse which they call love; but this love of theirs is firstly also the result of certain crystallized consequences of the properties of the same Kundabuffer; and secondly this impulse of theirs arises and manifests itself in the process of every one of them entirely subjectively; so subjectively and so differently that if ten of them were asked to explain how they sensed this inner impulse of theirs, then all ten of them—if, of course, they for once replied sincerely, and frankly confessed their genuine sensations and not those they had read about somewhere or had obtained from somebody else—all ten would reply differently and describe ten different sensations.

"'One would explain this sensation in the sexual sense; another in the sense of pity; a third in the sense of desire for submission; a fourth, in a common craze for outer things, and so on and so forth; but not one of the ten could describe even remotely, the sensation of genuine Love.

"'And none of them would, because in none of the ordinary beings–men here has

An Introduction to Gurdjieff

there ever been for a long time, any sensation of the sacred being-impulse of genuine Love. And without this "taste" they cannot even vaguely describe that most beatific sacred being-impulse in the presence of every three-centered being of the whole Universe, which, in accordance with the divine foresight of Great Nature, forms those data in us, from the result of the experiencing of which we can blissfully rest from the meritorious labors actualized by us for the purpose of self-perfection.

"'Here, in these times, if one of those three-brained beings "loves" somebody or other, then he loves him either because the latter always encourages and undeservingly flatters him; or because his nose is much like the nose of that female or male, with whom thanks to the cosmic law of "polarity" or "type" a relation has been established which has not yet been broken; or finally, he loves him only because the latter's uncle is in a big way of business and may one day give him a boost, and so on and so forth.

"'But never do beings-men here love with genuine, impartial and nonegoistic love.

"'Thanks to this kind of love in the contemporary beings here, their hereditary predispositions to the crystallizations of the consequences of the properties of the organ Kundabuffer are crystallized at the present time without hindrance, and finally become fixed in their nature as a lawful part of them.

"'And as regards the third sacred being -impulse, namely, "essence-hope," its plight in the presences of the three-centered beings here is even worse than with the first two.

"'Such a being-impulse has not only finally adapted itself in them to the whole of their presences in a distorted form, but this maleficent strange "hope" newly formed in them, which has taken the place of the being-impulse of Sacred Hope, is now already the principal reason why factors can no longer be acquired in them for the functioning of the genuine being-impulse of Faith, Love, and Hope.

"'In consequence of this newly-form-ed-abnormal hope of theirs, they always hope in something; and thereby all those possibilities are constantly being paralyzed in them, which arise in them either intentionally from without or accidentally by themselves, which possibilities could perhaps still destroy in their presences their hereditary predispositions to the crystallizations of the consequences of the properties of the organ Kundabuffer.

"'When I returned from the mountain Veziniama to the city of Babylon, I continued my observations in order to make it clear whether it was not possible somehow or

other to help these unfortunates in some
other way.

"'During the period of my year of special
observations on all of their manifestations
and perceptions, I made it categorically clear
to myself that although the factors for
engendering in their presences the sacred
being–impulses of Faith, Hope, and Love are
already quite degenerated in the beings of
this planet, nevertheless, the factor which
ought to engender that being–impulse on
which the whole psyche of beings of a
three–brained system is in general based, and
which impulse exists under the name of
Objective-Conscience, is not yet atrophied
in them, but remains in their presences
almost in its primordial state.

"'Thanks to the abnormally established
conditions of external ordinary being–existence existing here, this factor has gradually
penetrated and become embedded in that
consciousness which is here called "subcon-
sciousness," in consequence of which it takes
no part whatever in the functioning of their
ordinary consciousness.'"

That is a fairly typical passage. As you see, the
language is at first difficult, but it is an idiom to which
one becomes accustomed when reading it. At the
same time, I must warn you that this passage is
comparatively simple, compared with others, in the

Gurdjieff's Writings

number of new words used. The word "Kundabuffer" is invented, and so is the word "Sinkrpoosaram," but that is about all. There are other chapters where literally hundreds of strange words are used, so that at first glance a whole page may seem unreadable. But this difficulty quickly disappears and the relatively few important and necessary new words become familiar. In some chapters entirely new ideas are developed with regard to "work on oneself." This applies particularly to the chapter entitled "The Holy Planet 'Purgatory'," which Gurdjieff himself described as the heart of his writings. I must also mention the spirit of profound piety which pervades the whole book and of which you will have caught a glimpse in the extract I just quoted.

In some ways, the most significant feature of the philosophy which underlies the whole of *Beelzebub* is the notion of *universal fallibility*. The Universe is presented as subject to laws—but the very nature of these laws is that an element of uncertainty enters with the act of Creation itself. The history of the Earth is conceived in terms of a vast miscalculation which can only be partially remedied by intervention from "Above," that is by Messengers or Prophets sent by God Himself.

I have spoken mainly about the first two books of the First Series. The last part of the book consists mainly of criticism of the contemporary life of Europe and America. There are some very vivid pictures. As explained in the Introduction, the intention that Gurdjieff follows in this book is not to appeal only to

An Introduction to Gurdjieff

the mind, or even to the mind of feelings, but also to our power of visualizing and evoking concrete pictures for ourselves. Everything throughout the book is illustrated by stories and such pictures, even where very abstract principles are involved. These sometimes produce a most extraordinary effect, for example, a discussion on the nature of electricity and the nature of matter generally and of the higher energies in man is illustrated by a fantastic story of experiments carried out on the planet Saturn by beings living there who are supposed to have studied and understood the nature of this transformation of matter.

Nobody reading the book can fail to see that beneath all this strange mode of presentation, there is the very deep and serious standpoint that places in a much truer perspective than I think any other book of which I am aware, the human situation and the relation of Man to the Universe and to God. The book is not concerned with showing the practical methods of work, but at the same time, no one can read it attentively without finding out a great deal about this. From time to time, Beelzebub gives advice to Hassein as to what he should do, which we can easily see is applicable to our own work, our own states. When the whole narrative part of the book is finished, contained in forty-seven chapters, there is a postscript, called, "From the Author." This now leaves on one side the story of Beelzebub, and introduces and then quotes at length from a lecture presented by Gurdjieff in New York in 1924. This forms the transition to the Second Series in that, in this, there is introduced a great deal of material of the utmost interest and value connected with human psychology and the nature and destiny of man. Just to show you a bit about this transition, I am going to quote you what is called, "The Addition." When this lecture was given in New York in 1924, Mr. Gurdjieff himself intervened at a certain point and described human nature very much on those same lines as I described in the last lecture:

At this point, I interrupted the lecturer and considered it opportune to make the following addition:

THE ADDITION

Such is the ordinary average man—an unconscious slave of the whole entire service to all-universal purposes, which are alien to his own personal individuality.

He may live through all his years as he is, and as such be destroyed forever.

But at the same time Great Nature has given him the possibility of being not merely a blind tool of the whole of the entire service to these all-universal objective purposes but, while serving Her and actualizing what is foreordained for him—which is the lot of every breathing creature—of working at the same time also for himself, for his own egoistic individuality.

The possibility was given also for service to the common purpose, owing to the fact that, for the equilibrium of these objective laws, such relatively liberated people are necessary.

Although the said liberation is possible, nevertheless whether any particular man has the chance to attain it—this is difficult to say.

There are a mass of reasons which may not permit it; and moreover which in most cases depend neither upon us personally nor upon great laws, but only upon the various accidental conditions of our arising and formation, of which the chief are heredity and the conditions under which the process of our "preparatory age" flows. It is just these uncontrollable conditions which may not permit this liberation.

The chief difficulty in the way of liberation from whole entire slavery consists in this, that it is necessary, with an intention issuing from one's own initiative and persistence, and sustained by one's own efforts, that is to say, not by another's will but by one's own, to obtain the eradication from one's presence both of the already fixed consequences of certain properties of that something in our forefathers called the organ Kundabuffer, as well as of the predisposition to those consequences which might again arise.

In order that you should have at least an approximate understanding of this strange organ with its properties, and also of the manifestations in ourselves of the consequences of these properties, we must dwell a little longer upon this question and speak about it in somewhat greater detail.

Great Nature, in Her foresight and for many important reasons (about which theoretical explanations will be given in later lectures), was constrained to place within the common presences of our remote ancestors just such an organ, thanks to the engendering properties of which they might be protected from the possibility of seeing and feeling anything as it proceeds in reality.

Although this organ was later "removed" also by Great Nature from their common presences, yet owing to a cosmic law expressed by the words "the assimilation of the results of oft-repeated acts"—according to which law, from the frequent repetition of one and the same act there arises in every "world concentration" under certain conditions a predisposition to produce similar results—this law-conformable predisposition which arose in our forefathers was transmitted by heredity from generation to generation, so that when their descendants in the process of their ordinary existence established numerous conditions which proved to be congenial for the said law-conformableness, from that time on the consequences of the various properties of this organ arose in them, and being assimilated owing to transmission by heredity from generation to generation, they ultimately acquired almost the same manifestations as those of their ancestors.

An approximate understanding of the manifestations in ourselves of these consequences may be derived from a further fact, perfectly intelligible to our Reason and beyond any doubt whatever.

All of us, people, are mortal and every man may die at any moment.

*　　*　　*

If the average contemporary man were given the possibility to sense or to remember, if only in his thought, that at a definite known date, for instance, tomorrow, a week, or a month, or even a year or two hence, he would die and die for certain, what would then remain, one asks, of all that had until then filled up and constituted his life?

Everything would lose its sense and significance for him. What would be the importance then of the decoration he received yesterday for long service and which had so delighted him, or that glance he recently noticed, so full of promise, from the woman who had long been the object of his constant and unrewarded longing, or the newspaper with his morning coffee, and that deferential greeting from the neighbor on the stairs, and the theater in the evening, and rest and sleep, and all his favorite things—of what account would they all be?

They would no longer have that significance which had been given them before, even if a man knew that death would overtake him only in five or six years.

The passages I have quoted have perhaps conveyed a sense of undue emphasis in the description of the organ Kundabuffer in proportion to the whole. At the same time, it occupies a very important part in the exposition of these ideas—that is that man is not simply an incomplete being, who has something to do in order to become complete, but he is a being who has, as it were, his hands tied behind him. He begins with a handicap. He is unable to see things as they really are and therefore has not a fair start, and for this reason must have help.

In the concluding pages Gurdjieff turns towards the future and sets down the task which confronts those who have realized their responsibility towards coming generations. Everyone who is prepared to make the prodigious effort required must be prepared to sacrifice all personal comfort and all personal aspirations in order to become a Master to his fellows—a master who is the servant of all and whose authority rests solely on his greater capacity for effort and self-sacrifice. The last page sets down Gurdjieff's intentions with regard to the publication of his

An Introduction to Gurdjieff

writings. It gives a hint of the most intimate and personal style of writing which he will adopt in the Second Series:

It is now still midday, and as I have given my word that I would not, beginning only from tomorrow, write anything further for this first series, I still have time and shall not be breaking my word, if I add with a clean conscience that a year or two ago, I had categorically decided to make only the first series of my published writings generally accessible, and as regards the second and third series, to make them not generally accessible, but to organize their distributon in order, among other things, to actualize through them one of the fundamental tasks I have set myself under essence–oath; a task which consists in this: ultimately also to prove, without fail, theoretically as well as practically, to all my contemporaries, the absurdity of all their inherent ideas concerning the suppositious existences of a certain "other world" with its famous and so beautiful "paradise" and its so repugnant "hell"; and at the same time to prove theoretically and afterwards without fail to show practically, so that even every "complete victim" of contemporary education should understand without shuddering and know, that Hell and Paradise do indeed exist, but only not there "in that world" but here beside us on Earth.

After the books of the first series have all been published, I intend for the spreading of the contents of the second series, to organize in various large centers simultaneous public readings accessible to all.

And as regards the real, indubitably comprehensible, genuine objective truths which will be brought to light by me in the third series, I intend to make them accessible exclusively only to those from among the hearers of the second series of my writings who will be selected from specially prepared people according to my considered instructions.

Now we can turn, rather more briefly, to the books of the Second Series, *Meetings With Remarkable Men*. These are written in a form which is about as different as possible from *Beelzebub*. They are personal and autobiographical. They describe very simply the story of Gurdjieff's own childhood, the remarkable men whom he met and from whom he derived the point of view and the knowledge and the understanding of methods and so on, on which his own System has been based. It starts with his own father, his first tutor, and continues to describe his travels in different countries, the formation of a small group called the "Seekers of the Truth," which I

An Introduction to Gurdjieff

referred to in the second lecture. The chapter entitled, "My Father," is deeply informed with filial piety that finds its counterpart in Ouspensky's description in *In Search Of The Miraculous* of Gurdjieff's last visit to his father's home.

I referred in the second lecture to the influence of the Dean of Kars. I may quote a short passage from the chapter entitled, "My First Tutor."

I also very well remember that on another occasion the father dean said:

'In order that at responsible age a man may be a real man and not a parasite, his education must without fail be based on the following ten principles.

'From early childhood there should be instilled in the child:

> *Belief in receiving punishment for dis-obedience.*
> *Hope of receiving reward only for merit.*
> *Love of God—but indifference to the saints.*
> *Remorse of conscience for the ill-treatment of animals.*
> *Fear of grieving parents and teachers.*
> *Fearlessness towards devils, snakes and mice.*
> *Joy in being content merely with what one has.*
> *Sorrow at the loss of the goodwill of others.*

Gurdjieff's Writings

Patient endurance of pain and hunger.
The striving early to earn one's bread.

These early chapters convey the conceptions of education and early training which Gurdjieff conceives to be necessary for the men and women of the future. The real force of the Second Series of writings consists in this: that throughout these narratives of actual travels and meetings with "Remarkable Men" there emerges a realization of what was actually involved in seeking and finding the knowledge upon which Gurdjieff's teaching is based.

Before attempting to give you an explanation of the aim and significance of the Second Series, I propose to quote you a typical passage describing one of the meetings. It is dedicated to one of Gurdjieff's life–long friends, Professor Skridlov, Professor of Archaeology at the Universities of Kazan and Moscow. This is a description of a journey which he and Skridlov made together going up the old River Amu Darya, formerly called the Oxus, where they went disguised—Gurdjieff himself as a Seïd, or descendant of the Prophet Mohammed, and Skridlov as a Hadji dervish, this being a Mahometan country. Their travels finally brought them into contact with a Father Giovanni, an old man living in a monastery in Kafiristan where they stayed for six months.

We lived there as we wished, and went everywhere in the monastery freely, except in one building where the chief sheik lived and to which were admitted each evening only those adepts who had attained preliminary liberation.

With Father Giovanni we went almost every day to the place where we had sat together the first time we came to the monastery, and there had long talks with him.

During these talks Father Giovanni told us a great deal about the inner life of the brethren there and about the principles of daily existence connected with this inner life; and once, speaking of the numerous brotherhoods organized many centuries ago in Asia, he explained to us a little more in detail about this World Brotherhood, which any man could enter, irrespective of the religion to which he had formerly belonged.

As we later ascertained, among the adepts of this monastery there were former Christians, Jews, Mohammedans, Buddhists, Lamaists, and even one Shamanist. All were united by God the Truth.

All the brethren of this monastery lived together in such amity that, in spite of the specific traits and properties of the representatives of the different religions, Professor Skridlov and I could never tell to which religion this or that brother had formerly belonged.

Father Giovanni said much to us also about faith and about the aim of all these various brotherhoods. He spoke so well, so clearly and so convincingly about truth, faith and the possibility of transmuting faith in oneself, that once Professor Skridlov, deeply stirred, could not contain himself and exclaimed in astonishment:

'Father Giovanni! I cannot understand how you can calmly stay here instead of returning to Europe, at least to your own country Italy, to give the people there if only a thousandth part of this all-penetrating faith which you are now inspiring in me.'

'Eh! my dear Professor,' replied Father Giovanni, 'it is evident that you do not understand man's psyche as well as you understand archaeology.

'Faith cannot be given to man. Faith arises in a man and increases in its action in him not as the result of automatic learning, that is, not from any automatic ascertainment of height, breadth, thickness, form and weight, or from the perception of anything by sight, hearing, touch, smell or taste, but from understanding.

'Understanding is the essence obtained from information intentionally learned and from all kinds of experiences personally experienced.

'For example, if my own beloved brother were to come to me here at this moment and urgently entreat me to give him merely a tenth part of my understanding, and if I myself wished with my whole being to do so, yet I could not, in spite of my most ardent desire, give him even the thousandth part of this understanding, as he has neither the knowledge nor the experience which I have quite accidentally acquired and lived through in my life.

'No, Professor, it is a hundred times easier, as it is said in the Gospels, "for a camel to pass through the eye of a needle" than for anyone to give to another the understanding formed in him about anything whatsoever.

'I formerly also thought as you do and even chose the activity of a missionary in order to teach everyone faith in Christ. I wanted to make everyone as happy as I myself felt from faith in the teachings of Jesus Christ. But to wish to do that by, so to say, grafting faith on by words is just like wishing to fill someone with bread merely by looking at him.

'Understanding is acquired, as I have already said, from the totality of information intentionally learned and from personal experiencings; whereas knowledge is only the automatic remembrance of words in a certain sequence.

'Not only is it impossible, even with all one's desire, to give to another one's own inner understanding, formed in the course of life from the said factors, but also, as I recently established with certain other brothers of our monastery, there exists a law that the quality of what is perceived by anyone when another person tells him something, either for his knowledge or his understanding, depends on the quality of the data formed in the person speaking.'

The Second Series of Gurdjieff's writings contains many such accounts of meetings and conversations with "Remarkable Men." Each chapter is generally devoted to one of the members of the group, "Seekers of the Truth," whose attitude and manifestations typify a characteristic mode of approach to this work. The stories of the journeys are themselves full of subtle teaching upon human relationship, upon the study of human nature and upon "work on oneself."

On the title page of *Beelzebub,* the aim of the Second Series is stated: "To acquaint the reader with the material required for a new creation and to prove the soundness and good quality of it." In order to grasp how this aim is achieved, it is necessary to distinguish between the outer and the inner life of man. The material required for a new creation enters through our outer world and is made one's own, "transubstantiated,"—to use a term often employed by Beelzebub—by work and struggle in our inner world. The Second Series is concerned with demonstrating that the necessary material can in fact be found in the outer world by those who are prepared to seek with sufficient persistence and determination.

By describing the "Remarkable Men" who participated in the search and the even more Remarkable Men whom they found and from whom they acquired

An Introduction to Gurdjieff

the "material for a new creation," Gurdjieff enables the reader to form his own judgment as to the significance and value of what was done. But this judgment must be based on *external* evidence, for *internal* evidence is only established by the work itself. For this reason the conversations and practical demonstrations in the course of which real knowledge was conveyed to the "Seekers of the Truth" are usually described in terms of the external incidents only. There are one or two exceptions, notably in the chapter devoted to Ekim Bey, a Turkish doctor and hypnotist, who was from boyhood a friend of Gurdjieff and for many years a member of the "Seekers of the Truth." In this chapter, a description is given of the meeting with a Persian dervish with whom they had many conversations. Gurdjieff recounts in some detail their first talk in which the dervish gives practical advice of the greatest interest and value in connection with right and wrong work with the physical body.

In most cases, notably in the accounts of his periods of study in various monasteries and brotherhoods such as that of Father Giovanni, Gurdjieff is silent both as to the contents and the methods of the teaching which they received. In several passages he undertakes that this inner aspect of their search will be made known in the Third Series. Altogether, in the Second Series there is very little reference to Gurdjieff's own inner world, that is to his own personal reactions to the experiences and adventures of the "Seekers of the Truth." These chapters give a vivid picture of his companions and their journeys

Gurdjieff's Writings

—but the reader looks at the scene through Gurdjieff's eyes and does not see Gurdjieff himself.

The Third Series follows just the opposite course. It is, through and through, *a personal record of inner experience*. It describes the events of Gurdjieff's life over a period of forty years. Some of these events are already known to the reader from the Second Series—or even may have occurred during the period of his own contact with Gurdjieff and his work. A new light is thrown on all that occurred, by the revelation of his own inner experiences. We see from these writings how there was, over the forty years of struggling, a gradual emergence and clarification of the aim and significance of Gurdjieff's own life. This is not stated explicitly, but the attentive reader can see how the conception of his own task passed through the stages of the necessity to *know*, the necessity to *be*, and the necessity to *do*.

The Third Series cannot be understood by someone who has not immersed himself in *Beelzebub* and *Remarkable Men*. But if this preparation has been rightly conducted the study of the Third Series produces on the reader an extraordinary direct effect on the decision and power to make these efforts to *work on oneself*. Certainly to my mind no one has ever before succeeded in transmitting in written form the nature of this inner effort which is required to such a degree as is done in this Third Series of writings. Of course, it is not concerned only with our own personal inner world, but very much also with our relationships with other people, with the conditions which govern the right and wrong works of groups of people seeking the same aim, and in a larger sense with what is involved in bringing into the world a positive force which will create a New World. You will understand that I cannot quote for you anything illustrative of the Third Series of writings, nor would it be right for me to go into them in any detail. Indeed, it would not be profitable if I did, because people who approach the Third Series externally do not see what it is they draw from it. They may be very much impressed or they may fail to see any significance at all, because it is not easy to convey what "work on oneself" really means. Most people have no inner life in the true sense of the term. Their activity is outward and inwardly they are passive. The great task before us all is to rediscover the true significance of the inner life of man—not for its own sake or to take refuge there from the tribulations of the outer life—but because it is only the man who is inwardly alive who can play his part in the great work which lies before us. One thing and one thing only can save mankind from destruction and that is to arouse people from the illusion that nothing exists and nothing matters but the outer life of man. Those who are sunk in this illusion live like animals and perish like animals. Those who begin to escape from it realize that *Life Is Real Only Then, When 'I Am'*. This is the secret of right living on this earth and it is the secret of immortality.

Those interested in pursuing practical understanding of the ideas presented in this book through the system which has been developed by J. G. Bennett from his studies with Gurdjieff, Ouspensky, and other spiritual teachers, should write to the author:

c/o The Stonehill Publishing Company,
38 East 57 Street,
New York City, 10022

Other books by and about Gurdjieff:

The Herald Of Coming Good	G. I. Gurdjieff
Beelzebub's Tales to His Grandson	G. I. Gurdjieff
Meetings With Remarkable Men	G. I. Gurdjieff
Life Is Real Only Then When 'I Am'	G. I. Gurdjieff
Views From The Real World *—Early Talks 1918–1934*	G. I. Gurdjieff
In Search Of The Miraculous	P. D. Ouspensky
Our Life With Mr. Gurdjieff	Thomas de Hartmann
Undiscovered Country	Katherine Hulme
The Unknowable Gurdjieff	Margaret Anderson
Venture With Ideas	Kenneth Walker
Boyhood With Gurdjieff	Fritz Peters
Gurdjieff Remembered	Fritz Peters
Gurdjieff—A Very Great Enigma	John G. Bennett
Gurdjieff—Making A New World	John G. Bennett

Publisher's Note

The Publishers, with Mr. Bennett's permission, have included the Author's Inaugural Address to Students of the Second Basic Course (1972/73) at the International Academy for Continuous Education, Sherborne, England, as an Appendix to the paperback edition of *Is There "Life" On Earth?/An Introduction to Gurdjieff.*

This lecture first appeared in the March 1973 issue of *Systematics* Magazine (*The Journal of the Institute for the Comparative Study of History, Philosophy and the Sciences*), available from the Sales Editor, *Systematics*, 5-7 Kingston Hill, Kingston-upon-Thames, Surrey, Great Britain, by yearly subscription of $10.00 or at $2.50 per copy.

INTERNATIONAL ACADEMY FOR CONTINUOUS EDUCATION

Inaugural Address to the students of the
Second Basic Course 1972/73

John G. Bennett

Why have we come together and what do we hope to do in the year we shall spend together? There are two questions to be answered here: One is what kind of person we want to be, and whether we can find the means here of making a step towards becoming that kind of human being. The other is what kind of a world do we want to live in—for ourselves, our children, and our children's children. Can we find here the way to make some contribution to creating that world? If there were not both of these questions to be answered, I think I would not be here: I would not feel that it was my duty to devote my declining years solely to help you become a particular kind of person, though this is an important and necessary task. It is because I have the conviction that it is even more important the we should turn our attention to the kind of world that we want to see, to live in, that I am here and am ready to give the whole of my powers, as far as they go, to helping you to find an answer to your own questions. I hope also that we shall go some way towards an answer to the question we all must share; that is, what kind of a world are we going towards, and can we do something to make it more like the kind of world we want to live in?

151

Appendix

The kind of person that each one of us wants to be is really his own business. The choice is left to us. This is what it means to be a man. He has the power to choose what kind of a being he is going to become, what kind of a life he is going to live. That kind of being is rather rare in the universe. Most are allotted tasks in the cosmic order and they are formed in such a way that they have to play their part in it. Failure for them can only be failure of the environment to provide them with the conditions. An acorn will become an oak; it will become nothing else but an oak, providing the environment allows it. A lamb will become a sheep. A worm will become a worm. These are all serious cosmic roles that have to be filled. Without trees, without sheep, without worms, this Earth would not be able to fulfil its destiny, and the same is true of all the other kinds of beings. There are also, I am sure, beings of a higher order than man, who are also allotted tasks and they too are formed in such a way that they will fulfil these tasks according to a higher will with comparatively little choice as to what they themselves will be. This may be so because their task is of such importance that it has to be filled just as it is allotted to them. But we men are different. We men are confronted with the power, each one of us, to decide what kind of a human being we are going to be. All of us have an ideal and hopes for what we will become—but we know precious little about how to achieve it, and how to equip ourselves to fill the part that we would like to fill. Until a person has awakened perceptions that enable him to see it, even the path he has to follow is hidden from him. A peculiar thing characterizes us: Every human being has a cosmic role to fill, and we don't know what it is. We do not know how to prepare ourselves for it, and yet inwardly everyone of us—and especially everyone of us gathered together here—has a deep conviction that there is something we have to do with our lives. Each one of you knows that there is something that you have to find out about yourself and what you ought to be, and something that you need to know about how you become what you ought to be.

It is very strange that man should be put in this predicament, convinced that there's something important that he ought to know about himself and about the way he should be living his life, yet a veil is drawn which hides from him a great part of what he most needs to know. All the guidance he has is the past history of mankind, the ways in which people have lived before us, the way they thought it right to live and the way that they laid down that people ought to live. In most stages of the Earth's history, this will pass fairly well, but˙ moments come when it no longer works. Circumstances are changing profoundly, and the old precedents, the old traditions, the old rules and commandments no longer apply in the way that they have been understood before. These transitions have occurred over and over again in human history. They are moments of very great interest and significance, when the search for the ability to fill one's own role becomes more significant than at any other time.

We are in such a period of history when our inadequacy becomes painfully obvious. We know this, but do not understand why there is this deep feeling which everyone shares, whether they are willing to admit it or not. It is there, whether we hide it from ourselves and from others successfully or not. Deep down we know that something is missing. This makes us afraid; afraid in front of other people, in front of the world. Again we try to hide this fear from ourselves. This is the real crux of our situation: we know that something is not quite right, or something is missing but we do not know what it is. We put the best face on it. We do not know how to find this out. This does not mean that we do not also know that there is much we can do to change our situation. We know very well that there is much to learn, that we need to get more control over ourselves, more understanding and more sympathy with other people. We know that we are the slaves of many undesirable habits and we would like to correct these things, but there is something deeper. It is the awareness that we are called to something that we are not able to respond to. In this there is no difference between people except in the degree to which they can turn their backs on this situation and forget it and live without facing the question. For such people it is the outer world that is the trouble. If things go wrong, it is because of other people, because of circumstances, because of misfortunes, or at the most, because of mistakes that they make because they have not seen what to do. But those mistakes that they acknowledge are still well outside the real deep awareness that there is something in us that is missing. People who are able to live in this way, without concerning themselves with the deep question, can, in one sense, be called fortunate because they are free from the torture that people have to suffer for whom this question begins to burn. They can be very effective, they can be successful in life and they can convince themselves that their success satisfies them. They can do this in other people's eyes. They can see that they are admired, imitated, and with that they feel that they have evidence that all is well with them. But, as they grow older the time comes, perhaps moments come, when this question reappears

Appendix

for them, and that is no joke, because they see that the time for finding an answer to it has passed. But there are many, many people for whom the question does not arise at all and who go contentedly to the grave, thinking that they have made a success of their lives. And in one sense they have. Perhaps that is what they were intended to do, and perhaps that is the role they were intended to fill. It may be even that the inability to be aware of the deep questions was given to them to enable them to fill the role.

Let us take it that we who are here do ask this question and that we know that we will not be satisfied if we cannot find something more to do with our lives than making a successful impact on our society. One thing we shall try to do in this Course here is to reach the point where we can face this question together and begin to see for ourselves something which cannot be conveyed by words or explanations but only by an inner vision of the emptiness in us and how we are to pass through it and find the Reality that is beyond it. If I can help you towards this, this will be the most important achievement possible. A fair proportion of the people who came last year were able to do this, and this is more comforting perhaps than when we started a year ago, when I was obliged to say to everyone that I could not tell whether what we were setting out to do could be accomplished in ten short months, because I had never seen it attempted before.

I believe that it can be done and that those of you who have the necessary qualities and aptitudes can hope to achieve it. Others may not come to it this year, but if you are well-grounded you will come to it later.

I have spoken of the deeper significance of our work. This will not arise at first. There is much to be prepared and the preparation itself is progress. The work is traditionally divided into three phases, which we call the exoteric, mesoteric and esoteric phases. By exoteric, we mean coming to terms with the outward problems of our own nature, coming to know ourselves as human machines, to know how our bodies and our feelings and our minds work, and learn to some extent how to control ourselves. In this phase we also set ourselves to understand the principles which are true for us all. Those can be conveyed by talk or by illustration, by experiments of different sorts just because they represent part of the world in which we all share and which is within reach of our knowing power. If this goes fairly well according to pattern, it will take two or three months.

154

After that, we come to the mesoteric phase, when we seek to penetrate more deeply into our own nature and begin to understand for ourselves how it is that we are not in touch with our own reality. This is a matter of seeing. We in our modern English usage take the word theoretical in an abstract sense—but in old Greek *theoria* means a way of seeing that was objective as distinct from the ordinary subjective *opsis*. The divine seeing in us has to be awakened. Then we begin to be able to face the real problem, and see that it is this very thing which is the cause of the fear of people and their lack of confidence in themselves, which makes them timid or bombastic, active or passive, dominates them from behind the scenes without them being aware of it, and produces in them all the foolish manifestations of man. We see that facing this is the gateway to reality, and so far from fearing it, it is through that gate we have to go.

Those who can—and this I have no means whatever of predicting whether any one or ten or even most of you can do that—will come to the point where they will enter the world of Reality. This is called the esoteric phase. Whether this takes ten months or ten years does not matter. If it takes a whole lifetime, but is achieved in the end, that is a successful life in the objective sense. It is successful not in the external, visible sense, but in the cosmic sense, a life that has awakened to Reality and learned how to live in that world. Such a one becomes a cosmic being of a different order from ordinary men and women. It would be absurd to suggest that we could do more than put our feet on this path during this year. But if we achieve that, it is then for each one of us to follow it if we can.

The other question I put to you is: "What kind of a world is it that we want to see? What kind of a world would we wish to live in, to see coming for our children and our children's children?" From this standpoint, it is not my life or your life that matters, it is the life of mankind, of our children on earth who will come after us. There are probably not many of you here—I doubt if there is a single one—who thinks that this world in which we are living at this moment is an acceptable world that we would wish to have if we had the power to choose. There is something very wrong with it. One reason why the world is wrong is, of course, that the people who live in it now are not facing reality. They are facing reality neither in themselves, nor in the world of events. Matters that require to be looked at in the time scale of centuries are pushed out of sight. Matters that must be looked at in the scale of decades are disregarded. People live

155

for the moment. We stumble from crisis to crisis, and the larger the organization, the worse is this tendency to avoid facing the big issues and deal only with the small things. I learned this lesson fifty-two years ago when I happened to be interpreter to a peace conference and had to stand behind all the big men of the age—President Wilson and Lloyd George and Clemenceau and Sforza and all the people who were determining, as they thought, the future of the world—and saw with my own eyes how these great men of the world were moved by petty jealousies, unworthy personal considerations, even by sex and money. At the very time I was seeing all this in front of me, I was also going, whenever I could, to the lectures Ouspensky was giving, in which he was saying: "Man cannot do. Man has no control over his destiny. Man doesn't understand himself what is happening to him. He is a machine. He is asleep!" And it was strange for me to see, during the daytime, how everything I had heard from Ouspensky the previous evening was being verified before my very eyes. Soon we began to verify it all for ourselves. We saw how far we were from being the kind of person that we imagined or that other people assumed that we were. We saw how unwilling anyone is to face the reality of it all. But there are more specific things we can see in this world. One trouble is that people are the slaves of their feelings and are not able to act from their reason. They are not able to make compromises, accept difficult and embarrassing situations according to sane reason, simply because their feelings are too weak. Minds become the slaves of these weak feelings of theirs and the result is that they go from one trouble into another, from the inability to grasp nettles and be prepared to be stung a little in order not to incur a great deal of harm.

We live in this world, by the very nature of existence—not just the economy of this earth, but by the nature of all existence in space and time—in a state of corporeal limitation. We are limited by the fact of living in a body where everything is measured in quantities. There is one inescapable fact and that is that the things that *can* happen are very much fewer than the things that *might* happen; and, therefore, all that *could be* never *can be*. This translates itself into the simple proposition that *there can never be enough to go around*. Because we men have a great power of adaptation, if we choose to use it, there could be enough to go around if only we were prepared to discipline ourselves very severely and not grasp at everything we could take. We all know only too well that the world is not going that way, not by any means. And wherever there is power there is grasping. Nobody is really willing to give. They are unwilling to give way, owing to their emotional weakness, to fear, because they fear to lose something. They have become attached to quantity and do not see that quantity has no significance and that the reality is all qualitative. Value is not in the "how much?", but in "how real?" You have all come here thoroughly conditioned, by this grasping world. You have, unconsciously to a great extent, been conditioned to disregard the needs of others and to think only of yourselves. This is visible in the way you behave here. If you are not willing to struggle with this and to get free from it, what kind of example can you set to the world and how can we have anything which would appear to show what the world could be? In this place and time we have a world in miniature. When this course was being organized, I had to study the letters and reports of a large number of people who asked to come here. In accepting you I tried to arrange it so that we had people as varied as possible, with varied ages and varied types, varied positions in the world. And on the whole it has worked out like that. We wanted to have children and we have children, even more perhaps in proportion than the world has of children. In this little world, then, that we have here, we have to ask ourselves if we are going to try to live according to a pattern in which it is possible for man to live satisfactorily; a pattern which embraces all people, not just you and me. That will be possible only if we deny ourselves. We are going to make the experiment of putting ourselves on exactly the same plane as others, and never looking for more for ourselves than for someone else. The world must little by little be brought to understand that any other way of life will only produce conflict and eventually disaster. What can we do? If we can satisfy ourselves that it is possible to live this way, and we can taste for ourselves the satisfaction of living in that way, then we shall be entitled to speak to people and say that the world's present way of living is not the way of the future. My own experience of life has been that when I have given way and allowed myself to be imposed upon, it has always been good for me. Whenever I have refused to give way and tried to get things as I wanted them, it has always been bad for me. This experience has grown over a long life.

There are situations we shall study very soon, which I mention now because they concern the basis of our work. One of these is that one cannot be a satisfactory human being so long as one is dominated by likes and dislikes, by attraction and aversion. Such reactions are

157

Appendix

foreign to the true nature of man, who is not a polarized being, pulled
in different directions by external forces. Yes—no, like—dislike, active
—passive; these, called in the Bhagavad Gita the pairs of opposites, are
so central to the possibility of becoming a normal human being that
I speak about them in this introductory talk. If you are not prepared
to do everything you can to struggle with your slavery to likes and
dislikes, then it is little use for you to be here. In the ordinary way
of life we do the things that interest us and reject the things that do
not interest us. For example, if you go to college, you will probably
go to the lectures that interest you. If a course is dull or if something
does not interest you, you keep away from it. Here we ask you to do
quite the opposite: to do particularly the things that you do not like
and that do not interest you and, if you have to put everything aside,
to put aside the things that do interest you and that you do want to
do. If there are people here to whom you feel attracted and other
people in whom you do not feel so interested or attracted to, then
we would ask you to turn your attention to these latter. If there
are jobs to be done that you would prefer to avoid and jobs that you
would like to do and that fascinate you in some way, then give special
attention to the jobs you dislike and try to do them very well. I shall
say this to you yet again and I am speaking from long experience
which has shown me that nothing is more profitable in the stages of
this work that lead one to the threshold of reality than working against
likes and dislikes. If you are not prepared to do this and do not
remember it constantly, you will be wasting your time here. There will
be, of necessity, activities that do not interest you. Everyone will be
tempted to say: "Well, that particular subject or that particular lecture
does not interest me—now is the moment for me to go off and do
some shopping or go off and mend my clothes," or something of this
sort; or just simply, " I will have a rest because I am tired." Can
you bring yourself to say, "No, this one which does not interest me
is the one I will go to and the one that interests me is the one that
I will sacrifice."? If you do that, you will make real progress in what
matters; that is, in your own being, in your own real self. You must
remember that you are not coming here to be interested. You are not
coming here to learn subjects which will be useful to you. You are
coming here because you wish to be a real human being. And a real
human being is one who is free—and one who is not free is not
human. It is a special privilege and characteristic bestowed upon
man that he has the right to be free, but he has to earn it. And he

is not free, if he is the slave of his likes and dislikes. Of course, I do not mean by this that there is nothing useful to you all to be learned here. We hope very much that you will go away with many unexpected skills that you did not possess previously. You will be taught many things connected with the body, with the feelings and with the mind. You will come to see the way they work and much deeper things that are not in the ordinary sense knowledge at all but a direct inner vision of *what is*. Various things are arranged so that there will be opportunities. For example, let us suppose that something is made available in a quantity which is enough for everyone if each takes only his or her own share; then, if some people take more than their share and

others have to go without, we shall have a picture of how the world is. Let us say some food is put out to be taken which everyone wants to eat and enjoys and it is right that they should, but, if those who come first take more than their fair share and those who come last do not get any at all, then you are repeating the characteristic behaviour of the whole world at the present time. Everyone who can take takes; those who cannot take, who have not the power to take, are left empty. That is the way of the world. We must remind ourselves that the world we wish for is a just world. If we wish for a just world, then all our own actions must be just. Slaves cannot be just, only free people can be just. We shall have special opportunities of looking at the world situation, and we shall spend the last five or six weeks before we go, preparing ourselves for the work we will do when we leave here—to make use of what we will have come to understand and what we will be able to do.

Let us just take one of the aphorisms that Gurdjieff put up in the Study House in his Institute, and which is also true here, namely that *here we can only create conditions; we cannot do your work for you.* And another thing that was written in the Study House was: *You have come here to struggle only with yourself. Be thankful to anyone who gives you the opportunity to do so.* I look around and see a lot of nice faces. I think it would be very much easier if there were a few real monsters here. We have all of us got a monster hidden somewhere, so that maybe we can manage without any imported monsters. What I have just said—that nobody can do your work for you—you have to take to heart. This is not an easy way. It is not easy to be responsible for oneself. It would not be so difficult if I were simply to make hard conditions which you would have to bear and feel very proud that you were able to bear our conditions, or if I were to behave like a monster and you were able to say, "Well, I can bear with him because he cannot be too monstrous for me." I have seen enough of that kind of thing myself to know that it doesn't really get us where we need to get to. The work has to come from within. It has to come from our own need, our own decision. Try to remember this: it is not easy. We shall have to work hard. And we do have a wide range of activities from all kinds of practical work. This has been arranged and we have every opportunity of doing practical things. Some of the people in last year's course said they felt sorry for you because you wouldn't arrive in a stone-cold house with the kitchen ceiling collapsed and only one broken-down stove to cook for a hundred people. They feared that you wouldn't know what the life here was like. I don't think that that is really necessary every time. We have got the Stable Block in front of us as a challenge and we have a lot of work to do both inside and in the garden. Every one of these jobs provides an opportunity for working in a positive way: acquiring skills, improving attention, of learning to work with other people, learning to work on all your functions—all the things that are useful.

In addition to this we will do a good deal of work on the movements. These are beautifully designed for developing not only the bodily powers of man, but his complete balance of mind, body, feelings and will. As much as possible, the theoretical background will be covered in the psychological meetings you will have with Dick Holland. Every week when we have our morning meetings, I will be showing you different exercises to work at and providing you with a theme for working on understanding together. We have a meeting tomorrow morning when I will put before you the first theme for the first week and on Friday evening we will begin to talk about what you have found in studying this. I shall also be taking various special subjects. I intend to repeat what we did last year in teaching you a language. I debated whether to teach Turkish or Sanskrit: there would have been interest in being able to recite the Gita in its own

language, or to learn some of the magnificent Vedic hymns. But there is more value in Turkish from the point of view of communication, because it is totally different from our European languages. Also, I am glad to say that I have been able to arrange with Henri Bortoft, who is a man of exceptional genius, to give two courses in Hermeneutics. The first will start fairly soon and most of you have asked to have the opportunity of working with the Alexander people with whom we are arranging to come here. So we shall have a very varied programme. I shall be bringing other experts in for some specialized work. So it won't be a lack of interesting things to do; but there will be, I hope, and I think we shall achieve it also—some uninteresting things to do. We'll give you the opportunity of doing things because you dislike them, not just because you like to. If we can't come to the point where all people are the same and we have no more difficulty in making friends, with or talking to, Mr. X than to Mr. Y, where we have no barriers between us and different kinds of people, and where we have no barriers between us and different kinds of activity, where it's all the same thing to be a dustman or a prince —unless we attain that, we are not free.

Gurdjieff
Making a
New World

by John G. Bennett

With *Gurdjieff: Making A New World,* John G. Bennett has attempted a mammoth task—to place Gurdjieff's life and work in
its true historical perspective and to effectively relate the significance of his three-volume *All and Everything* to his mission.
Certainly the most important study of Gurdjieff's Ideas since
Ouspensky's *In Search Of The Miraculous,* Bennett sets out to
enquire whether the teacher was simply an isolated phenomenon
or, rather, one aspect of a cultural tradition that has for centuries
influenced and been concerned with the destiny of mankind. His
remarkably original presentation of Gurdjieff's world view also
describes the varied and colorful methods adopted by Gurdjieff
to transmit his teachings. Bennett's painstaking researches into
Gurdjieff's early life and the sources of his Ideas give the book a
solid foundation while the study is held together throughout by,
what the author refers to as, "Gurdjieff's Question": 'What is the
sense and significance of life on the earth and, in particular, of
human life?'

320 pages. 15 Illustrations plus maps. $8.95
Available in March 1974 from Harper & Row.

Order from Dept. GM, Stonehill, Box 978, Edison, N. J.
08817, enclosing check or money order for $8.95 plus 50¢
postage and handling.

John G. Bennett

Photo: Annette Green

Mathematician, scientist, linguist and author, John G. Bennett was born in 1897 and has, for fifty years, been actively working to pass on to others the Ideas of Gurdjieff and Ouspensky. Bennett first met Gurdjieff in Constantinople in 1920 and attended his Institute for the Harmonious Development of Man at Fontainebleau near Paris for a short period of time in 1923. Back in London, he took instruction from Ouspensky for two decades before once more rejoining Gurdjieff in Paris after World War II. Bennett remained in close contact with Gurdjieff throughout the last years before the teacher's death in October, 1949. Since then, he has been associated with many other spiritual leaders, including Shivapuri Baba and Idries Shah, and is presently Principal of the International Academy for Continuous Education in Sherborne, Gloucestershire, England. Bennett's newest work, perhaps his most significant to date, will be published by Harper & Row in Spring 1974: *Gurdjieff—Making A New World.*

George Ivanovitch Gurdjieff
(1877-1949)

Since his death in 1949, the influence of
this extraordinary mystic philosopher and
teacher has continued to make itself felt to an
ever-increasing degree. His unique teachings
—on the many psychological problems sur-
rounding Man, his potential, and his relation
to the Universe—and his novel methods for
practical self-development—devised in large
part from traditional techniques and tempered
for the twentieth century western world—
have gripped the attention and concern of
very many people. A number of these have
been popularly recognized over the years as
ones who have reached the zenith of their particular fields of endeavour. Indeed, Gurdjieff's
work and ideas embrace and have come to
fruition in all possible areas of true human
accomplishment.

Many have been brought to the teachings
by the lectures and writings of such well-
known exponents as P. D. Ouspensky, A. R.
Orage, and M. Nicholl. Others have come by
way of curiosity and interest sparked by the
current profusion of memoirs recounting various periods and diverse aspects of Gurdjieff's
long and colorful career. More have been introduced to his system by Gurdjieff's own writings, which exist under the collective title, *All
and Everything*. And, of these, many have been
provided with their first initiation into the
practical work by pupils of Gurdjieff—of
whom J. G. Bennett is one—to whom he entrusted his methods and who continue to actively transmit them to serious students, young
and old and from all races and walks of life,
throughout the world. Besides the certain interest of *IS THERE "LIFE" ON EARTH?* to
the many already acquainted with Gurdjieff's
revelatory ideas, this will serve as a dramatic,
pointed and lucid introduction for the ever-
growing number of seekers who are, in Gurdjieff's words, "hungry for *something more*."

1924